# MORE LOVE
# (LESS PANIC)

JEREMY P. TARCHER/PENGUIN

*a member of Penguin Group (USA)*

*New York*

# MORE LOVE (LESS PANIC)

*7 Lessons I Learned About Life, Love, and*

*Parenting After We Adopted*

*Our Son from*

*Ethiopia*

CLAUDE KNOBLER

JEREMY P. TARCHER / PENGUIN
Published by the Penguin Group
Penguin Group (USA) LLC
375 Hudson Street
New York, New York 10014

USA · Canada · UK · Ireland · Australia
New Zealand · India · South Africa · China

penguin.com
A Penguin Random House Company

Most Tarcher/Penguin books are available at special quantity discounts for bulk purchase
for sales promotions, premiums, fund-raising, and educational needs. Special books
or book excerpts also can be created to fit specific needs. For details, write:
Special.Markets@us.penguingroup.com.

Library of Congress Cataloging-in-Publication Data

Knobler, Claude.
More love, less panic : 7 lessons I learned about life, love, and parenting after we adopted
our son from Ethiopia / Claude Knobler.
p.        cm.
ISBN 978-0-399-16795-9
1. Intercountry adoption—United States.    2. Intercountry adoption—Ethiopia.
3. Adoptive parents—United States.    4. Adopted children—Ethiopia.
5. Interracial adoption—United States.    I. Title.
HV875.5.K616        2015                    2014027018
649'.145—dc23

Printed in the United States of America
1   3   5   7   9   10   8   6   4   2

*Book design by Gretchen Achilles*

*For Mary, Clay, Grace, and Nati*

*The best part of my life is being a part of yours.*

# CONTENTS

# MORE LOVE
# (LESS PANIC)

I WAS FAR FROM HOME, AWAY FROM MY WIFE AND KIDS, SITting in a dusty café in Addis Ababa, between a woman I'd never met and our five-year-old son, who didn't speak a word of English.

Now, years later, my family looks very different from most. I have a son and a daughter who have lived their whole lives in Southern California and I have another son who spent the first five years of his life in Africa. My eldest son and my daughter grew up going to birthday parties at the beach and at Disneyland. My youngest child once was chased through his grandmother's home by a stray hyena. As I said, my family is different than most.

This book is not about that.

This book is not about how my family is different than other people's families because at heart, we are the same. I have learned many lessons since the day I sat in that café in Addis Ababa, but they were not lessons about how to parent a child who was different than me. They were lessons about how to parent all of my children. The only thing that's different about my family is that sometimes the differences we shared made the lessons I learned stand out a bit more clearly.

Because my son was five years old when we met, I learned that it was far better to influence my kids than to try to control them. Because my son didn't speak any English, I learned that I wasn't very good at worrying, no matter how much I practiced. Because my son spent his first five years in Africa, I learned about perspective and seeing life through my kids' eyes. Because every day of raising my son presented new challenges, I learned that not nearly perfect was, actually, more than good enough.

I will never forget the day I met my son, just as I will never forget the day any of my kids came into my life, no matter the circumstances. I was already a father, twice over when I met my son and his mother in that dusty café in Addis Ababa.

I didn't know it at the time, but I was about to learn everything I would ever need to know about being a parent.

To all three of my children.

# IT'S BETTER TO INFLUENCE THAN TO CONTROL

*How Nati's Mother*

*Taught Me about*

*Letting Go*

ONE DAY, MY WIFE AND I DECIDED TO ADOPT A CHILD from Ethiopia, in spite of the fact that we had two perfectly good children right in our very own home.

We had our first child—our son Clay—when we'd been married for two years; our daughter, Grace, was born about two and a half years later. One boy, one girl, and that was that. Or at least that was the plan. I'd never wanted more than two kids. Truth was, raising two kids kept my wife and me so busy that sometimes it already felt like we had a dozen. And adoption was never something we'd considered or even discussed, except in the vaguest "we really ought to do something for the world, like adopt a needy orphan or sell all of Clay's and Grace's toys and give the money to the homeless" sort of way. The first time I can really remember my wife and me even really discussing the idea was after I'd read an article in our Sunday newspaper about the AIDS crisis in Ethiopia.

The story was straightforward. "What Will Become of Africa's AIDS Orphans," by Melissa Faye Greene, described how the AIDS epidemic in Ethiopia had left countless children orphaned and in need of care. I suppose I've read a lot of articles over the years that were similar to that one in some ways, but this was different. The way that story was told moved me in ways that no other story had.

That was my first lesson.

So much of parenting seems to be about control. My children were six and four years old. Because I was a stay-at-home dad, I was in charge of feeding them, dressing them, and getting them to bed at night. *In charge.* Because that's what parents expect to be. In control. It was, I believed, my job to make my children into successful, intelligent, kind, thoughtful adults capable of professional and personal excellence. Also, my wife wanted grandchildren. But not too soon. I was well meaning, determined, and focused on doing my job as a parent as it was possible to be. After all, I was in charge.

And yet when it came to one of the most important life-changing decisions I'd ever make, I was more or less carried along by the current. The paper came. I read an article. I said a few things to my wife. My life changed forever.

EVEN THOUGH MY LIFE was simpler before our third child came home to us, it often felt more complicated. I worried about Grace's nap schedule and the all-important question of whether she was getting enough midday sleep. I worried that Clay was far too cautious during recess. Why was he more interested in exploring the cracks on the pavement than in the basketball games being played all around him? Was he aggressive enough to succeed in the world? And what about the food they ate? Clay was a picky eater. Grace wasn't all that fussy, but still I worried. . . . Living in Los Angeles, where almost everyone we knew had at some point dealt with body issues, had left me worried about how to feed my kids. I wanted Clay to eat enough so he'd grow, but I didn't want to put out so much food every day that I somehow wound up contributing to Grace's developing any kind of problems later on in her life. It seemed to me then that every choice I made could and would forever determine not only what sort of lives my kids would have but who they would forever be. My life felt more complicated than it does now—not because it actually was more complicated but because I was convinced that my every action could, if properly executed, ensure that my children would lead lives of unending good fortune and success. My life felt complicated and burdensome because I was trying to carry more than anyone really could. I was, in many ways, like a man complaining about how heavy his car is, because he's trying to lift it instead of just getting in and driving.

And then the Sunday paper came.

I read that story that I'd found buried between the sports sections and the front page. I gave the article to my wife and then, after she'd read it and had a good cry, I said, almost casually, "You know, we could adopt a kid from there."

And here, I have to be honest. I've gotten a lot of compliments about deciding to adopt. My favorite, I think, was when my sister said, "You know, you could rob a bank or two and still go to heaven." I'm very proud of what my wife and I decided to do. But the truth, the absolute 100 percent real truth of the story, is that I never ever thought my wife would do it.

It's not that I didn't think my wife was a good person. She

was and is. It's just that Mary and I already had a full life. We had our two kids, who we adored, friends, family . . . pretty much everything we needed. We weren't looking to add anything to our life, except maybe, since our kids were both so young, a bit more free time. Maybe some naps. But another kid? No way.

Mary and I had met about ten years before that magazine article. I had been complaining to my friend Paul that my life felt dull and predictable. Paul wisely told me that if I was bored, I should start doing things that scared me. And so, since I was single, I decided I'd try asking out the prettiest girl I saw at a party I was going to, whoever she turned out to be. That was Mary. I got her phone number, and not long after, Paul got to be my best man at our wedding. When I tell my kids now that I fell in love with Mary just ten seconds into our first phone call, I always think that I must sound ridiculous, but it really did happen that way. I fell in love that quickly and I never fell out.

We were married a year after we met, and we had our son two years after that. Two more years passed and we had a daughter. We had two kids, two dogs, and each other. We had the usual difficulties parents of young kids have, the ones that come with not sleeping a full night for months and years at a time, but I've never really gotten over the happy surprise I felt when I realized that someone like Mary wanted to be with me.

Still, as wonderful as I think Mary is, I was pretty sure I

was in the clear when I gave her that article. Because I knew there was no way she'd be crazy enough to say yes.

Bragging rights. The high ground. A slight bit of moral superiority over my wife. These are the things I was really after. A child? Not so very much.

No, I'm not proud to say it, but the truth is, I was just looking to score some cheap points. My plan was to say we could adopt a child and then have Mary think it over before deciding that having another kid would just be too hard on us. I would go along with her decision.

But, of course, Mary would know. Always. Every time I forgot to put my dishes in the dishwasher, every time I decided to stay home and watch a game instead of going to brunch with her family . . . she'd know that I was the sort of guy willing to do remarkable and wonderful stuff, if only, you know, she'd have let me. I'm not saying I made the offer to adopt a child from Ethiopia just so that my wife couldn't give me a hard time when I blew off taking out the trash, but yeah, that was a part of it, and, sad to say, it's not even the worst part.

The worst part was that I knew she'd tell our friends about how I was ready to adopt a needy orphan. I'd mention it casually to a few people too. Word would spread about my offer. And yes, when I died, I would probably go to heaven, even if I did decide to rob a bank or two. Was I genuinely moved by the article? Of course. Had I given some actual thought to the idea of adoption? Some, sure. Do dogs ever think about what it would be like to drive the cars they chase? Could be. But in my case, it never, ever occurred to me that my wife would say yes.

It was such a good plan.

How lucky am I that it didn't work?

Say for a moment that the paper hadn't come that week, or imagine that I'd spilled milk on the magazine section and thrown it out before I'd read it. I truly believe to the core of my being that my whole life, and the lives of my kids, would have been forever different. I had never planned on adopting a child. I had never considered adopting a child. Even when I suggested we consider adopting a child, I wasn't really considering adopting a child.

Believe me when I say there were days, weeks even, when I thought the only lesson I'd learned was not to read the Sunday paper. That Nati was from Ethiopia, spoke no English, and was a total stranger to us at age five was, in some ways, the least of the challenges he presented. Day after day it was made clear to me that Nati not only looked different from me, but he *was* different from me. Louder, sillier, more assertive. And so I began to find that I had to change and evolve as a parent in order to keep up with him. But it was because we were in such an extreme situation that I began to see what parts of my parenting style worked and what parts didn't. Eventually, because of all my struggles to parent a son who was so different from me in so many ways, I realized something that was to forever change the way I parented and the way I lived.

I don't want the last word.

It was, for me anyway, counterintuitive. Having the last word feels like a parent's right, obligation, and duty. We can see so much that our kids can't see. We know how much better off they'd be if they worked just a little harder. We understand that the boy or girl they like is all wrong for them. We know that if they only did a few more things after school, ran for class president, joined a club, learned to play the tuba, or cured just one tiny little disease, they'd get into a better school and be better off forever. We know more than they do. When I was growing up, the last words of so many arguments with my parents tended to be, "Because I said so."

"You'll do it because I said so, because I know best and that's the way it's got to be." And so we demand the last word. Do your chores. Share your toys. You must follow our curfews and rules and expectations. Because we know best. Because we said so, that's why. Oh, and one day, you'll thank us. Because when you're a parent you'll understand. Sound familiar?

And yet we all know that we can't really control quite as much as we'd like to control. No matter how much better we'd be at living our children's lives for them, kids insist on making their own choices. Whether it's a kid picking the wrong boyfriend, college, or best friend, or just refusing to practice the flute no matter how much it may increase her chances of going to an Ivy League school one day, we are continually confronted with the limits of our own power.

It's not much of a choice, or at least it doesn't seem to be. Either we can let our kids make their own rotten choices (and let's not fool ourselves, children do make some really rotten choices) or we can live in conflict with our kids, butting heads and demanding that they do what we say no matter what. We can condemn ourselves to ten or fifteen years of arguments and misery in our own homes, or condemn our children to a lifetime of mediocrity and the sorts of diminished options you get when you drop out of the rotten college you got into because you didn't study hard enough for your SAT in order to marry the loser you stayed out with because you didn't have a curfew. On the left, misery; on the right, despair . . . which is it to be?

It was that Sunday paper that showed me the third way. It took a good long while; a trip to Africa, a child and a woman I tried with all my heart and cowardly soul to avoid meeting, but eventually it became clear enough so that even I could see it. That third way, the way of having the first word instead of the last, is what I learned after I adopted that child I hadn't planned on actually adopting. I had to find it in order to stay sane with that kid from Africa who looked and acted so differently from my wife, my two other children, and me, but to my surprise that third way wound up working with all three of my kids, the one I adopted and the two I already had. This book is about that third way and all the mistakes I made along the way. But first, well, first the paper came.

I didn't spill my milk on it. I read a story and made a kind of sort of casual comment to my wife about kind of sort of maybe adopting a kid. Someday.

And then we did.

June 2, 2004

Dear Mary,

I'm being charged only 3 birr per minute to use the hotel computer; that's about thirty-three cents to you and me, but I'm not feeling all that well, so I'm still going to make this pretty quick. Nati is sitting on the floor by my feet, singing a song in Amharic and doing a coloring book. He sings all the time. This morning we both got up at around 6:30; I'd actually been up most of the night, but he gave me a big smile when he woke up and scooted over for a hug. We tried to watch some TV, and hung out. He watched an Arabic version of *Sesame Street* and some *Barney*. Later we caught the tail end of the movie *How the Grinch Stole Christmas*. After that, we had some trouble. There's a bidet in the bathroom and he started to turn on the water. I said "no" then left the bathroom. When I came back he had turned it on and flooded the floor. I gave him a big NO and then took him into the bedroom. He cried and wouldn't make eye contact to talk to me, so I just let him cry and sulk for a few minutes while I cleaned up the water. Then I said, "Daddy say no, Nati no, not Nati yes . . ." or some other such gibberish. Anyway, I think he got the message. Or not, hard to say. He has a lot of willfulness. He smiles and wants to get along, but then he does what he wants anyway.

Oh Mary, I'm sorry I'm not doing a better job of telling you everything that goes on, but I'm so tired and a bit sick and this keyboard is killing my wrists and . . . and . . . I don't know, I'm really looking forward to coming home. This has been really hard, tiring, and emotional. I guess it's like childbirth; you know it's going to hurt, you just can't really prepare for it. But Nati is a good boy and I think he'll do fine, or at least I think that when I'm not in a crazed panic.

As for Ethiopia, I'm with your friend Sara, I'd be very happy to never ever come back. The hotel is stunning, but there are tin huts just across from the big beautiful hotel driveway. The people are poor, it's not a safe feeling being outside; all in all I'd have to say I'd have rather adopted a kid from London.

And Nati is still at my feet, singing and coloring in his book. He holds my hands all the time, is very affectionate, loves, loves, loves the light-up sneakers we got him, loves elevators and oh, he really dug the Silly Putty I brought him. I thought I'd be able to do that Silly Putty trick where you copy a comic onto the Silly Putty and then stretch it out, but it didn't work with the Ethiopian paper or his coloring book. He didn't know the experiment had failed though so now he just happily pushes the Silly Putty down on the paper for no reason at all. Plus when we were watching TV I didn't know what channels he wanted. He kept saying some Amharic word, like din, so I asked, "din yes? or din no?" making a face so he'd know what I meant. Now every time I switch channels he says, "din yes, din no."

Okay, soon I'm off to the Hilton to confirm my reservation for the flight home. I really, really don't want to get bumped off the flight, which I hear sometimes happens on flights from Ethiopia.

Did I mention I love you and miss you more than I can ever say?

And I am now being treated to an Amharic version of Ring around the Rosie.

Life is a very odd thing.

I love you, I love you, I love you, and I love you some more.

Love,
Claude

To my surprise and alarm, Mary said that maybe thinking about adopting might be a good thing. And so we began. Slowly and tentatively. Just enough to change our lives forever.

It's funny. When you decide to have a kid the usual way, you really ought to know that you're not in charge right from the start. You don't normally get to pick whether your child will be a boy or a girl; you have no say in their hair color, height, or personality. It's a roll of the dice. Looking back, I know that by the time we had Clay and Grace, I was already making plans for who I'd "help" them to be, but even with all my hopes/expectations about their futures, on some level I knew I had no idea what I was getting into.

With adoption, we literally were going to get to choose our child. Which should have meant we were in control. And it's true that because we'd read an article about orphans in Ethiopia, Mary and I had decided that if we adopted, we would adopt a child from that country.

Both of us have been asked why we didn't simply adopt a child from our own country, and both of us have answered that question with a series of very honest shrugs. There are needy children everywhere, but for us, it was always clear that either we would adopt a child from Ethiopia or we wouldn't adopt at all. Perhaps it was the article we read; perhaps we'd been called in some spiritual way; perhaps we just wanted to rule out 99 percent of the globe so that if we didn't find a child from Ethiopia to adopt we'd be off scot-free, but there it is; for us, that part of it was easy. We dealt with one adoption agency and focused on the children in one country. If nothing else, through the process of geographical elimination, we'd made choosing a child, if not easy, then at least easier.

Now all we had to do was decide if we really were going to adopt and then, who? The choice, after all, was ours. Right?

My love,

Well, it's 1:45 pm here, which means you're fast asleep, so I can't call, so you'll have to settle for e-mail.

Today we went with our guide Salemech to the open market, which was pretty unpleasant. There were lots of beggars, as well as young boys herding goats through the main streets. Salemech told me that people will just stop and buy a goat to bring home to kill for dinner. At one point a mule ran down the main road of the market place, something which I can't quite imagine happening at our local mall. Apparently its owner felt it needed some exercise. Or maybe he thought I needed the exercise, I just barely managed to sprint out of the mule's way before it ran me over. People were selling shoes as far as the eye can see, old shoes and old clothes. Not much you'd want to buy, but it was sooo good to be out of the hotel. Nati was very sweet and well-behaved. In fact, he's with me now, watching me type this with great fascination. He's a really sweet guy, at least he seems to be, with the language gulf, he may be walking around calling me "dufus" all day. Anyway, after the big market we went to Churchill Road to buy some junk/remembrances and that was very nice. Churchill Road is what, I guess, would pass for upscale here, it's really just a fairly calm street, with a few goats but no runaway mules. There are a bunch of little storefronts that sell little statues of lions and jewelry to tourists. Nati got a musical instrument thing, which he loved and was very proud of and I bought all sorts of stuff for Clay and Grace. We even stopped at a little coffee shop, so that Nati could have some "dabo and chai," bread and tea. I passed on the pastry for myself though, I haven't been able to hold down the thought of food for a few days now. Then we went back to the hotel, he colored, I was sick, we had some soda, it was all very nice. (I think that's the upside of being in a place where mules run wild down the main streets; I now think of getting sick as just a chance to be alone quietly for a few minutes.)

Oh, and remember the green windbreaker jacket you made me pack? He's wearing it, complete with the hood, right now, even though we're inside. Very cute.

I love you.

Me

Going to Ethiopia to see the kids in person before deciding which, if any of them, we'd adopt, was pretty much out of the question. We knew of only one other couple who'd gone to Ethiopia to select which child to adopt, and that was second-hand. A woman who'd gone to pick up her new daughter had run into a very blond, very cheerful couple who were, it seemed, working their way through some of Ethiopia's many orphanages, "interviewing" various kids for the job of being their son or daughter. Forget the cruelty of raising and then dashing so many children's hopes of finding a loving family, and you're still left with the problem of what can you possibly learn about any child when you're standing in the middle of an orphanage surrounded by dozens of kids, none of whom speak English, all of whom are desperate to find new homes.

We also knew a family that, having chosen a child to adopt, went to Ethiopia before the adoption became official to check out the kid, but they'd regretted it. Once you've chosen your child, there's a wait period of about five months; the family had told the little boy he was going to be joining their family, and then the father had flown out to meet his son. Satisfied that the child was not a homicidal maniac and would fit in well with the rest of the family, the father returned to America alone. His son, having met his new father, then had to wait five months to join his new family, which, in the end, proved to make things only harder for everyone.

So instead of traveling to Ethiopia, we watched videos.

Hi Mary,

I just got back from the goodbye party at Nati's orphanage. I don't want to spend too much time typing, Nati's with me, of course, and I want to let him chill for a bit before we meet little Des, Nati's friend from the orphanage, and his new mother, Dr. Jane, for dinner but I did want to give you some quick impressions of the party.

Dr. Jane was oohing and aahing over the orphanage and how all of the caregivers loved and knew all of the kids, but I have to say for me, with nothing to compare it to, it was pretty dismal. The classrooms are tiny, little shacks really. My head almost touched the roof. The kids seem okay, though it's pretty crazy, of course. (And right now, in case you're wondering, Nati is by my side singing up a storm. He's a real Knobler, not happy unless he's talking.)

I brought those balloon rockets to the orphanage, they were a huge, huge hit. For a while there it was like Beatle mania. I'd blow up a balloon, kids were all around me, then I'd let the thing go and they run after it. I actually had to stop when it got too crazy. I took tons of photos, it rained a bit, but everyone was excited to pose for pictures and then see the image on the digital screen.

I don't know what else to say, I'm overwhelmed, but Nati seems so happy and at ease with the idea of having a whole new family that I now fear he may be psychotic.

Anyway, the orphanage, though wonderful by Jane's standards, seemed crowded, dirty, and awful, but then, compared to the rest of the country, it's not so bad.

Okay, gotta run, Nati is bugging people here with his singing. Guess I'm off for a two-hour private concert.


Love,

Claude


SOMETIME BEFORE THE INTERNET MADE dating as easy as logging on to GuysWhoLikeTallWomenWhoLikeWaterPoloAnd MerylStreepMovies.com, there was something called video dating. Single men and women sat in front of a camera; talked about themselves and their interests, what they liked and what they didn't; and then paid a small fee so that other single people could look at their tape. When two people liked each other's videos, they made a date. Oddly enough, what we did to adopt a child was not all that different from video dating.

Once a month, the orphanage in Ethiopia sent out a tape to an agency here in the United States featuring as many as fifty children. The agency sent the tape to our house; we then would watch the tape to see if any of the children featured were someone we'd want to adopt. There were, of course, differences; unlike in video dating, we were talking about a lifetime commitment and not whether we'd agree to go out to dinner and a movie, and yet, unlike in video dating, there was not much talking on the tape. Each child appeared on our screen for perhaps ten or fifteen seconds, just long enough for them to smile and then say their age and name.

The names were all foreign-sounding, of course; nothing that, for me anyway, gave any comfort. As foolish as it may sound, tell me that you know two children, one named Jim and one named Stanley, and I can't help but think I know something about them both. But Dagwit? Wendimu? Kidist? I was desperate to know who they were, but with names like those, I felt wholly and totally lost.

Because some of the girls had short hair, I often found myself having to ask if Wendimu was a boy, if Kidist was a girl. Their ages meant little; often the children didn't know how old they were and were simply guessing. The smiles were painful to see: eager, hopeful, desperate, and, no matter how energetic, sad. And the more energetic the smile, the sadder the effect. I had the power to actually choose my child, so why did I feel more powerless than I'd ever felt before?

Mary and I watched the videos. Sometimes with Clay and Grace, sometimes just the two of us. After a while, I stopped watching every tape that came in. A package would come in the mail, I'd hand it to Mary, and she'd watch it alone. Later, if I remembered, I'd ask if there was anyone special on the tape that I needed to see, and she'd just shrug. I have no idea how many children we looked at on those videos. A hundred? Two hundred? We had no idea what we were looking for, nor did we have any idea how we could possibly make such a huge decision.

After watching one tape, we thought seriously about choosing an older girl. The woman holding the camera said the girl's name and age, then mentioned that she loved reading and wished she could have more books. We'd decided before seeing any videos that we wouldn't be adopting a child who was older than Clay, or a girl of any age. Our thinking was that adding a new child to our family would be hard enough without changing Clay's place as the oldest kid or Gracie's as the only little girl in the house. Then again, perhaps we were just trying to make the decision through the process of elimination. Still, we wavered as we thought about all of the books we owned, all of the books Clay and Grace had. We thought about that girl's life in Ethiopia. We thought about . . . everything. Could she share a room with Gracie? Would we be up to the challenge of parenting a girl who was older than our kids, but could not express herself in English any better than a toddler? Would she boss around our two younger kids?

We watched her on the tape a few times. She seemed shy. Maybe she was quiet and bookish. Or then again, maybe she was a deranged sociopath whose favorite authors were Stephen King, Edgar Allan Poe, and the Brothers Grimm. We hesitated, and then without really ever talking about it, decided that we would not adopt that girl after all.

In time, over the course of a year, I stopped believing we'd ever choose anyone. We saw siblings and knew we weren't willing to adopt two or three children at once. We ruled out older girls and all babies, since I had no interest in sleepless nights spent with crying infants. Boys older than Clay were out too, but there was no way we could really make a choice through process of elimination alone. There were what seemed like an endless amount of young boys that we could have chosen to adopt . . . but didn't. They looked into the camera, said their names, told their ages, and we just did nothing. *Perhaps*, we thought, *we're just fooling ourselves. Perhaps we really don't want to adopt.* Why not that child? Why not the one in green, the one with the nice smile? Another month, another tape, another group of children.

The problem seemed to be unsolvable. Mary began trying to raise money from people at work for orphanages in Ethiopia; it seemed more and more to us that we might help out that way instead of adopting. We began to feel relieved. We wanted to help but felt we were just destined to be off this particular hook.

Because she was trying to raise money for adoption-related causes, Mary was now in contact with the adoption agency's director. We were, we told her, "good, but not that good," our way of making sure that she knew that we were not looking for anyone who had any extra challenges. One day, the director told Mary that she thought she might know of a little boy we might like. A week later, a small postage stamp–sized picture arrived in the mail.

Control is a funny thing. When your kids are young, it's easy to feel as if their lives and destinies are in your hands. Making your child split a cookie in two so he can give half of it to his sister becomes a crucial opportunity to mold your son's character and turn him into a compassionate, generous person. Putting your daughter on the "right" nap schedule seems like a make-or-break chance to help her grow into an independent young woman who can comfort herself and will therefore be less likely to date the wrong guys. We live our lives as parents as if we are driving a car. We see ourselves as masters of our kids' fates, determining their destinies with every turn of our steering wheel. We know what sort of people we want our children to become, and so we map out a route to get them to where we think they need to be. The fact that we don't always seem to be in control of our lives doesn't in any way make us suspect that we can't manage and control every element of children's characters, fates, and destinies.

But what if we're not? What if we're not driving a car at all but are actually passengers on a train, headed to a destination that we can't choose or control? What would it mean if we weren't really in charge of the things we thought we were? What then?

The boy in the photo was not, to my mind, especially cute or appealing. He was wearing what looked like two shirts and a jacket, odd given that he was, after all, in Africa, a place not known for its chill. His head was tilted downward, but his eyes were gazing straight ahead, which made him seem angry or, depending on how nervous I happened to be feeling about adoption when I was looking at the picture, malevolent.

The picture we'd been sent sat in our kitchen for a few days and then made its way onto a pile of bills, unmailed letters, and invitations to kids' parties in the small room that I used as an office in our house. And there it stayed for a few weeks. It wasn't a letter to be mailed, or a paper to be filed, and yet throwing it away seemed oddly cruel. Whenever Mary or the kids came into the room to interrupt a phone call, they'd look at the picture, along with the party invitations and bills. None of us said, "I don't like the looks of this kid," nor did anybody say, "By Jove! He's the one!" I began to wonder when I should toss the picture and whether anybody would notice if I did.

Another video came, with a note telling us to look for the boy in the picture. We all sat down and started watching. The boy in the picture was the first kid on the video; Mary and the kids began shouting, "That's him! That's him!"—I thought because they'd recognized his face from the photo. A moment later, though, they were still shouting, "That's him!" but in a different tone. The first "That's him" was the four of us saying, "That's the boy in the picture." The second was different; it was the sound of our lives changing forever. Somehow in that second, Mary and I had become the parents of three kids. That was him.

I'd like to tell you why that picture was different from all the others, but I can't. It just was.

The boy in the picture was standing against a wall. Someone spoke to him off camera. The boy in the picture looked disgusted with whoever was speaking off camera and made a motion with his hand almost as if to push them away. Then, in the video, he laughs, sticks his tongue out, and then is gone. Another boy comes on the video next, then a girl, then a few dozen more kids.

We all looked at each other, laughing and feeling amazed; was that the one? Is this how you feel when "you just know"? We asked the woman who ran the orphanage for any news about the boy in the picture. We learned that his name was Nati, that he was five, that he'd just been brought to the orphanage, that he seemed in good health and good spirits, that he was born on October 31, 1998, and that if we wanted to adopt him we'd have to make our decision in the next few days so that other families who might be interested as well would be able to pick him if we decided not to.

Looking back, I know that our choice had already been made. We'd seen the boy who was our son. And yet . . . we stalled. We churned it over in our heads.

And then, we made our two young kids figure it out for us.

Yeah, that last part is not something I'm proud of.

The boy in the picture, we decided, was fine with us, but only if our kids both went along with the idea. I like to think that we made at least some effort not to put it that way to Clay, then seven, or Grace, then five, but I can't swear that I didn't. Certainly it strikes me now that if nothing else, I'd given them something really big to hold over their brother on days when he wouldn't share some of his dessert with them: "Excuse me, but I was the one who said you could come here in the first place." It wasn't my best parenting moment, but sometimes you can only do what you can do.

Gracie was a pushover; to her adopting a child was like getting a new puppy. She thought the boy in the picture was cute and that getting to be his sister would be fun, case closed. Indeed, she was so sure that she wanted to adopt that we immediately discounted her opinion. We turned to our son.

He was, he told us, not 100 percent sure that adopting the boy in the picture was the right thing to do, and he said he needed time to think it over. We let him know that we were under a bit of a time crunch. No serious pressure, mind you; we just need you to decide the fate of another human being living thousands of miles from us. Nothing any seven-year-old couldn't knock off before lunchtime. Seriously, that's pretty much when I kissed any chance of ever winning the Father of the Year Award good-bye once and forever.

Clay decided that he'd like to call a few friends to get their reactions. Understand that up to that time, I had never seen Clay speak on the phone for longer than fifteen seconds. My parents or sister would call, I'd ask Clay if he wanted to say hello, he'd agree, and then, like a vaudeville actor, he'd say the word *hello* and then pass the phone back to me.

We asked Clay who he wanted to call. He gave us the names of a few friends. We told him that sounded like a great idea but reminded him that this wasn't something he could put up to a vote. It was fine to ask what people thought, but in the end, this still had to be a private decision. Then, having told him that he couldn't let other people make his choices for him, we dialed up a few numbers and let our kid talk with a bunch of other seven-year-olds to see whether we'd be adding another human being to our family. Forever.

And let me just say again, yeah, not a great moment for me as a father. Do you think maybe you could stop sighing so much? Honestly, I can hear you from here.

Most of our friends by now knew that we'd been considering adopting for some time, so perhaps it didn't seem too bizarre when we phoned them and told them that our son would like to speak to their son about whether we should adopt a child. Then again . . .

Clay called four or five children that night. We could hear only one side of the call, but here's what it sounded like:

Clay: "Hi, Morgan? It's Clay. My family is thinking about adopting a kid. Do you think we should? [Short pause. Way too short, by the way. Just long enough for some kid to look up from whatever video game they happened to be playing and say, 'Uh, yeah,' or 'No, I wouldn't.'] His name is Nati. I don't know. He was born on Halloween, isn't that cool? Yeah. Okay, bye."

Clay would then turn to us and say, "Morgan thinks we should."

"Ah," I would say.

"Good," Mary would add.

And then we'd call the next kid.

There was one thing Clay said in each of his calls that seemed to really impress all of the other children and that, I can quite honestly say, may have swayed the majority of voters. Nati's birthday was on Halloween. This was deemed by all to be "cool." Had Nati been born on Groundhog Day, he might now be living with some other family. Had he been born on October 29, he might not have been adopted at all. The Lord and his seven-year-old helpers work in mysterious ways.

After he'd finished calling his friends, my son announced that he was ready to adopt.

"Ah," I said.

"Good," Mary added.

We called the director of the adoption agency and told her that, yes, we would be adopting Nati. We didn't mention the part about how we really liked that he'd been born on Halloween.

Mary,

Better and better every day, I think, hope and pray. I'm sort of learning how to do this, not how to be a father to a child from Ethiopia, that's going to be a much longer process, but how to be a father here in a hotel in Africa. Room service, for example, is bad, it's far better for us to get out of the small room where there's too many fancy telephones and bidets and things he wants to play with but can't.

So, this morning we watched cartoons for a while, I took a shower, then we went to one of the hotel restaurants for breakfast. You wouldn't believe how confident this kid is, by the way. We stopped at the sundries shop for a minute and Nati and the woman running the place had a chat (which I, of course, didn't understand a word of, since they were both speaking Amharic. She had to translate it all for me later). He danced for a second and then said, "this is how to dance." We worked on saying good morning in English, he then told her speaking English was "easy." He's sitting by my feet now, drawing and singing. He's just so sure of himself, it's amazing.

I'm much less sure of myself, though. At the restaurant I had the hostess help me translate with Nati. Nati opted for pastries, which he didn't much like. He drinks tea in the morning and likes to dunk his food in his tea or drink (he once dunked a French fry in his 7-Up, but

I'm trying to wean him off that). Tell Grace we have another tea drinker in the family.

Today our guide comes at 9:30. I'm going to see about getting Nati a small haircut. He's got this mullet/ rat tail that I'm not crazy about. After the trim, we'll hit a museum, mostly just to have something out and about to do. Then perhaps, back to St. George's Church. Last time we went, we couldn't go in; they were having a service. I asked our guide how long the service lasted, thinking we could wait, and he said, "three hours." Every day. The guide said that people were so poor and had so little to do that they often went to the long services just to keep busy. There are just so many poor people with nothing to do here. Men lie down in the street, young kids just wander around or sit on the street doing nothing. Foolish fathers spend too much time in their hotels with five-year-old boys. No, wait, forget that last part.

Anyway, we'll stay out doing stuff as long as we can. I think I'm going to try and get our guide to eat with us, here in the hotel, then we'll go to the orphanage to meet Sara, the social worker, who'll take us to meet Nati's birth mother. I should be freaking out about that, but I find that everything I do here is so . . . so much, that I have to just do what's in front of me and nothing else. Being worried about Nati's mom would be like trying to breathe tomorrow, today. Don't get me wrong; I haven't gotten holier than thou, I do spend some time worrying about this whole deal, and how things will be at home, but mostly I'm just trying to stay afloat.

Still, Nati and I shared some genuine silly laughs today. He's a goofball, yet very well-behaved right now and at restaurants. He's a keeper, Mary, though this will be a hard process.

Okay, I'm off to be a bit sick, then to take Nati to his haircut. Pray for me today, I can't imagine what my afternoon will be like.

I'm very big into the praying these days, by the way, it's been so much help. I just keep begging for help and comfort and strength and amazingly it comes. I was really worried about how long it would take them to process Nati's visa so we could go home; I'd been remembering those stories about people who had to spend an extra two weeks here and I don't think I could have made the extra time. At one point, I got on my knees and said as much of the St. Jude prayer as I could. Remember when I got that St. Jude prayer card in the mail from that charity we'd never heard of? Patron Saint of hopeless causes seemed about right, assuming that He doesn't mind I'm Jewish and haven't too much of an idea about what I'm saying. Anyway, when the woman who was putting together Nati's visa asked me, "When do you want these?" it was very truly, for me, a prayer answered.

I know that these letters and calls have been a bit unnerving, but I do think this is going to be fine. I love you more than is humanly possible. Kiss the kids and give them such a squeeze from me.

Love,
Claude


The adoption agency told us that our first job as new parents and siblings was to fill a gallon-sized plastic zip-lock bag with small toys, a little photo album, and perhaps some clothes for Nati, as well as a note welcoming him to our family. When a child gets one of those zip-lock bags, they know they've been adopted.

We went shopping. We knew Nati was five (and that he'd been born on Halloween) but not much else. We bought some small cars, a toy plane, some stickers, and a shirt. We made a photo album. This is Clay, your brother. This is Grace, your sister. This is your new mom. Her name is Mary. I'm your dad. This is a picture of your new room and of all your new pets. It was as strange as anything I've ever done.

A few weeks later, we got another photograph. It was of Nati, the moment he'd gotten his zip-lock bag and he found out he had a new family, his face lit up with excitement. The bag we'd put together was on his lap; we all marveled that it had made such a long trip. We looked closely at the picture and tried to remember buying each of the toys we saw in the bag on his lap. We looked at Nati's beaming face. "Well," Mary said later on that night, "at least it looks like he's happy we adopted him."

We continued with the large amount of paperwork required in an international adoption. We were now receiving pictures of Nati from the orphanage on a fairly regular basis. Having no other information about our son, both my wife and I began to construct personality profiles for our new child, based on nothing more than the size of his smile in each picture. A photograph would come in the mail of Nati smiling and looking sweet and adorable. "He's shy," we'd decide; "he's going to be very quiet. He'll probably love to read. I hope it won't be too noisy for him here." Another picture would come; this time, there was no smile. "He's going to be an arsonist," I'd decide. "He's going to grow up hating me because I'm a big dumb white guy. He'll ruin Clay's and Grace's life when he kills our pets." Another picture: this time with a big goofy grin. Another personality profile.

Mary became an active participant in an online community composed of parents who had adopted or planned to adopt. People who were flying to Ethiopia to claim their children began sending us pictures and, more important, tantalizingly brief reports. We learned that Nati was "a charmer," that he was "sweet" and "silly," and that he seemed "smart." We tried to buy clothes and toys accordingly.

It was another four months before the Ethiopian govern-

ment gave me permission to come and get my son. We looked at pictures of him; we asked questions of people who'd gone to Ethiopia to claim their new children. Nati was, we heard, "cheerful." Other people told us he was "quite a handful." Breathing seemed to no longer be an automatic function our bodies did without needing to be reminded. We waited. I showed the picture of Nati to all of our friends. I began to realize that the child we had chosen was strikingly beautiful, though he certainly had not seemed all that handsome in the first photos and video we'd seen. Someone at the orphanage sent word to us that Nati liked cars. And volleyball. At the time it seemed like a wealth of information, though we were pretty sure that the part about him liking volleyball was, at the least, a bit of faulty translation.

It had been five months since we'd "chosen" Nati and a year since we'd begun considering adoption, and this is what we knew about our son. He liked trucks. He was cheerful, or at had been at least for a half hour when a woman we didn't know had seen him while picking up her own newly adopted child. He liked volleyball. Or didn't. Perhaps he'd just seen a volleyball once. He stuck his tongue out once at someone. He was born on Halloween. His mother was dying and could no longer take care of him. His father was already dead.

The only other thing we knew was that he was ours; that he would be in our family forever, would sit with us every night at dinner, and that one day, we might well be there to watch as he and his volleyball team took home the Olympic gold.

What we did not know was whether he was psychotic, if he was serious or silly, loud or quiet, mean or kind, a lover of books and stories or a hyperactive party animal.

We took to reminding ourselves that Nati was just a five-year-old boy and not Bigfoot; a small child in need of a home and not a rampaging monster with the strength of ten men. We took to noticing various kids who our children didn't like at school, bullies and mean six-year-olds, and wondered if we'd be stuck with one of them.

At long last, we were given a travel date and told we could buy airline tickets, arrange our visas, and get ready to go to

Ethiopia to get our son. After a good deal of talk, Mary and I agreed that she would stay home with Clay and Grace while I would go alone to pick up Nati.

None of the letters I sent Mary could ever really capture the experience of going so far away to such an impoverished country, to meet our son and to see his birth mother, dying of AIDS but still so very much in love with her boy. Each day I spent in Ethiopia was filled beyond capacity. I remember the days as a blur. I know that one day, I'd gone to see the orphanage Nati had been living in, met dozens of kids who had not yet found families, been ill a few times, held Nati down while a doctor removed some stitches my son had in his chin, been nearly killed by a runaway mule . . . and then had lunch. Still, I tried to get it all down, sending e-mails from my hotel, while Nati drew in a coloring book by my side.

Hi Mary,

It's 2 pm here, 4 am back home. I just got back from watching Nati's mom say goodbye to her son. I don't know what I can possibly say about that experience. We drove up to the same restaurant we met at yesterday. Nati's mother, grandmother, uncle and cousins were there, plus a few friends of Nati's mom. One of the cousins was able to tell me a few things about Nati's parents. They eloped; it seems Nati's maternal grandfather didn't approve of their getting married, though I'm not sure why. The cousin was on Nati's father's side, she said his father was "kind and funny." He used to play practical jokes on his sister, the aunt I met the day before. He'd dig holes to hide her stuff in and write things on her school stuff (or clothes, I'm not sure which) and get her into trouble. He loved Nati very much and wrote, "Nati" and "I love Nati," on the walls of his home while he was dying. He apparently had a bad car crash, got tainted blood transfusions and then died two years later. I asked if any of the people there, who all seemed to love Nati and dote on him, had considered adopting him themselves. She told me that they'd all talked about it, but decided not to since they wouldn't have been able to afford to raise him well and to pay for his education. I don't know anything about that. Better with us than at the orphanage in Addis Ababa he was living in the last six months.

I'm feeling pretty drained right now. Nati's mom cried, as did I. I told her through her cousin that you wanted me to especially let her know that we would always care for him, would make sure that he had every opportunity in life and would always let him know about where he was from and who everyone in his family was.

I guess the thing I'm thinking about a lot right now though is this. What made today so awful and so hard was that it was so ordinary; my guide told me he'd been to 20 such parties in the last bit of time, five in the last two months alone. Back home, when one of the kids has a playdate that gets canceled, we sit with them and talk about their feelings and help them as best we can, but here a family saying goodbye to one of their own isn't something to tarry over. I think that's what's been hardest about being here in Africa, the kind of jet lag that comes not from time zones, but from the over-whelming knowledge that we have everything, in dupli-cate, and they have nothing. The men here sit and lie by the side of the road, the kids have nothing. It's not that I don't think we should have those long conversations with our kids over canceled play dates either, hell, I can't wait to go home and have them with Nati, it's just that there's no honest way to cope or process when the tragic and desperate become commonplace. I think I could cry and cry but another part of me just wants to lie down by the side of the road. It's such a defeated city, I truly cannot fathom how anyone can come here and experience it as anything else.

God Almighty I can't wait to see you.

I love you.
Claude

WHEN WE WERE WONDERING how we could ever choose a new son or daughter for ourselves and how we would ever know whom to choose, there was one thing that people with experience told us over and over: "You'll just know."

"How will we know? How will we know if we're supposed to adopt anyone at all? And if we are supposed to adopt someone, how could we possibly ever know who that should be?" we'd ask.

"You just will," they'd always say.

It's strange but true, that the people who most understood how little choice is involved in choosing a child were the people who'd already done it. They seemed to have already realized that they never really were choosing someone at all. They were just waiting to find out who their son or daughter already was.

What nobody told me, and what I never thought to ask, was not *how* would I know, but *when* would I know. I'd assumed that I'd know when I saw my son or daughter in a video. I assumed I'd see his or her picture and that something deep inside me would click. And maybe it did; maybe I was just too panicked to hear it at the time. I don't know if I heard that click when we chose Nati from a ten-second video clip. I know I didn't hear it the first time I saw the boy in that stamp-sized picture of him. I do know I have heard it since then. Most of all, I know I heard it the moment I saw Nati for the first time.

I'd gone by cab to the orphanage. When they opened the gates, I saw a few kids coming toward my car. Nati saw me before I saw him. As soon as I got out of the car, he came to me; when I knelt down by him, he put his head on my shoulder and held me. I was his father now, and would be forever more. He knew it, and in that moment, so did I.

I hear it still, that click inside me that tells me Mary and I did the right thing, found the right child. Sometimes, it's during the quiet times. I heard it when he was younger when I tucked him in and he'd say, "Good night, Dad." Sometimes it's when we're all just goofing around together, or when I hear him laughing in the car with Clay and Grace. Nati is my son; we could not have chosen anyone else. I like to think we never actually chose him in the first place. I like to believe that we just found each other.

Mary,

I only have time for a short note right now, but I really wanted to tell you something. I was just walking down the hotel hallway with Nati. He ran ahead of me and then hid behind a wall. When I caught up with him he jumped out and then yelled the Amharic version of boo. We were laughing together afterwards, holding hands as we went to the elevator and without meaning to, I thought to myself, "Yeah, this can work." Anyway, I just thought you might want to know I've met our new son and that I like him.

Love,

Claude

We just knew.

In the end really, it was that simple. In the end, we just knew. Unfortunately, I spent the beginning and middle in a panic. And then, after the end, I panicked some more.

Lots and lots of panic.

Which actually, I think, sums up a lot of what we sometimes confuse for good parenting. Panic. Our attempt to find the right preschools followed by the right music teachers to help get our kids into the next right school so that they'll have perfect adult lives is really nothing more, for me at least, than a bizarre way to deal with the panic that comes out of the love

I feel for my kids. I love them so much, and want so much for them to be happy, all the time, always, that I get a little panicky. Because even as I do all those things designed to make my children just slightly more successful, happy, and emotionally well adjusted than any adult human I've ever actually met, some part of me realizes that it's not going to work. I know, on some level, that the cello lessons I want to get for a six-year-old won't really guarantee that she'll get into Harvard, become a doctor, and live an emotionally and financially fulfilling life, because I live in the world and I know that things don't really work that way. Six-year-olds get older and they grow up in different ways. They get interested in what they want to get interested in, and nothing I do when they're six is going to completely dictate who they'll be when they're sixteen.

Which is where the panic comes in. Trying to control the whole of another person's life and knowing that you can't possibly do that tends to lead to an unbalanced emotional state. How could it not? How can you want the best for your children without letting yourself go crazy trying to give it to them?

The answer was that I had to learn to let go. The question was how. Even the process of adopting Nati, all of which took place before I actually began raising him, made it obvious that I had to learn to stop trying to be in charge of things that I wasn't in charge of. Sadly, letting go is—for me, anyway—a fairly terrifying process. The love I feel for my children makes me want to hold tight, both literally and figuratively. It makes me want to take the reins of their lives firmly in my hands and force them into the futures I think will make them most happy. But adopting and then raising Nati has taught me over and over again that's just not possible. From the beginning, I found myself learning that if I was going to be truly loving, I was going to have to learn to accept him as he was, and not as I wished him to be. I had to learn to let go of the people I loved the most.

And yet . . .

And yet parents often do know best. If you are an adult reading this book, you are almost certainly smarter than a four-year-old, or, for that matter, than a fourteen-year-old. So what do you do?

I had to meet the bravest, saddest, most remarkable woman I've ever known to learn that answer.

When Nati was about four, his birth mother became too ill to continue to care for him and so, because his father had died when Nati was little more than a year old, she took him to live in a village with his grandmother. After six months, his grandmother, owing to age and not illness, was also unable to care for Nati, and so he was brought to an orphanage in Ethiopia's capital city of Addis Ababa. While he was in that orphanage, he did not see his mother, his grandmother, or any of his other blood relations. He stayed there for six months, until I flew out to bring him to his new home and his new family.

Before I went to Ethiopia, my wife and I were told that I would have "the opportunity" to meet Nati's birth mother so that he could say good-bye to her. There were two reactions among my friends and family to this news. The first was that this opportunity was a blessing, a wonderful chance to both learn about Nati's history and allow my new son to have a final chance to connect with his biological family. The second reaction was that this "opportunity" was dangerous, that it might prove traumatic to Nati, that it would be best to avoid any and all contact with Nati's birth family, and that what could be gained from such a visit would not be worth the efforts the visit would entail.

Those who had reaction number one, that the visit was a wonderful and blessed opportunity, included my wife, our friends, other parents who had adopted children, and the woman who ran the orphanage in Ethiopia. Those who had reaction number two, that the visit was a bad idea and should be avoided at all costs, consisted of me.

Yup, just me. No one else.

Mary, already feeling bad about not being able to come on the trip to get Nati, since, after all, someone had to stay with Clay and Grace, made it clear that she expected me to meet with Nati's mother and began asking other parents of children who'd been adopted to put together a list of questions for me to ask Nati's mother. Most everyone had a few suggestions. I was told to ask about Nati's medical history, his relationship with his birth father, and his general upbringing. I was instructed to ask for baby stories, favorite foods, and general likes and dislikes, and told to get as much of Nati's overall genealogy as I could conceivably gather. I, in turn, told my wife that I would definitely consider meeting Nati's mother depending on how things went while I was abroad.

I had two reasons for not wanting to meet with Nati's birth family. The first reason was the one I tended to talk about: my concerns that meeting with Nati's family would be traumatic for him. What if, for example, his mother had reached a stage in her illness where she was visibly ill; would it then be right to make his final and perhaps only memories of her mental images of how she appeared while sick? Would any five-year-old be able to process saying good-bye to his own mother? Would saying good-bye to his mother, in front of me, leave him always resentful, unable to bond with me or any of the members of his new family? Would it be just too hard for him?

The second reason was that I was scared out of my mind.

I was afraid it would be hard on Nati, hard on me, that there would be sobbing, weeping, and worse. I worried about the fact that Nati's mother was HIV-positive, I worried about being close to someone who I feared would be sickly and frail. In the end, there is no defense or explanation needed for that kind of fear; I had it, and that is all.

I first realized I'd lost my argument about not meeting with Nati's family during my flight to Ethiopia when I spoke with the woman who was going to adopt Nati's friend Des, Dr. Jane Aronson. Jane, who founded a well-known and widely respected charity called the Worldwide Orphans Foundation to benefit children, is known professionally both as Dr. Jane and the Orphan Doctor, though I sometimes prefer to think of her as Dr. Jane: The Orphan Doctor Who Is a National Authority on How Best to Care for Orphans and Who Knows More about This Stuff Than I Do. When not traveling around the globe providing medical care for needy children and running her charity, Dr. Jane: The Orphan Doctor Who Is a National Authority on How Best to Care for Orphans and Who Knows More about This Stuff Than I Do's job was to advise her patients, the parents of adopted children, in how to best care for their children's physical, mental, and emotional health.

So this taking-care-of-orphans thing wasn't just something she'd been, you know, dabbling in.

Dr. Jane and I chatted on the plane. We chatted about our soon-to-be sons, who, as luck would have it, were close friends at the orphanage. We spoke about our fears, our hopes, and the various difficulties we'd had in getting this far along in the process. Somewhere over the Atlantic Ocean, I hesitantly told Dr. Jane that I might be able to meet Nati's family but I wasn't sure that would be for the best.

"No," Jane said to me, "you have to."

Not, "You should," or "I think you'll be glad," but "No, you have to," spoken with all of the confidence doctors seem able to summon up whenever they are talking about what the rest of us should be doing.

Jane went on to tell me not only how important it would be for Nati, for me, and for my entire family, but how lucky I was. A couple she knew had adopted a son from Ethiopia with no living relatives they could visit. Since they were unable to visit any of their son's relatives, they'd gone instead to the area where the boy had briefly lived before he was placed in an orphanage. They'd taken photos of the streets and spoken to all of the people who'd met their son and interviewed them on videotape. Finally, they had found the name of a street corner where the director of the orphanage had told them their child might have once been seen, and they made a video of that as well. All this, Jane explained, because it was important to give a child as much information about where they'd come from as you possibly could.

I have never, to the best of my knowledge and memory, lost an argument so thoroughly.

After I'd met Nati and spent a day or two with him, I spoke with Sara, one of the women who worked at Nati's orphanage. I told her that I'd been informed I could meet Nati's mother and said I'd do so, if she thought that was for the best. Sara then contacted Nati's mother and a meeting was arranged at a restaurant not far from the orphanage.

I was terribly sick the first time I met Nati's mother. Honestly, I'd been sick the entire time I was in Ethiopia. The first few days Nati knew me, I was just a pasty white blur racing past him on the way to the bathroom.

Nati and I had left our hotel and gone first to Layla House, the orphanage for the older children, to pick up Sara (Nati had been living at another orphanage for babies and kids under five). You have to go through a locked gate to get into the orphanage, and there's a bit of greenery on the outside of the gate, so that driving up, it looked like we were heading into a comfortable-sized home or estate. Once inside, however, there was no lawn or anything green. The driveway was dirt; the first building looked old, faded, and worn down. Children came running out from all directions as soon as we pulled up, all wearing clothes that looked as if they'd never been new. We parked our car in the dirt driveway, then walked a few steps to the dirt area the kids play in. There was a small basketball hoop hung on a wall, near the office.

I waited while Sara dealt with a crisis, watched as Nati played happily, and took pictures. I was nervous, restless, and fairly desperate to use the restaurant's bathroom, having been informed in no uncertain terms that the bathroom in the orphanage was not a place I'd ever care to see, let alone actually use. We all finally got into my cab and drove off. When we pulled up to the restaurant, I saw Nati's mother and his aunt outside waiting for us, and everything changed.

I've thought about this, and as grotesque as the comparison may seem, the only time I have ever had such a sudden shift in perspective was in the first seconds of my daughter's life.

I had not wanted to have a second child, and had agreed to have another only at my wife's insistence. In spite of all my resistance, however, the moment I first held Gracie, I fell hopelessly in love. I suppose that's pretty common but prior to the day I met Nati's mother, I'd never felt anything else at all like it. One minute I'd been a reluctant soon-to-be second-time father, the next I was blissfully happy and head over heels in love. And though the circumstances could not have been more different, the feeling of everything changing was exactly the same. This was not the joyful occasion of my daughter's birth; I was there to let my son's mother say good-bye to her child. It was as sad a day as any I could imagine, but it was still a day of total transformation. I'd come to that restaurant nervous, nauseated, and filled with questions I was supposed to ask about Nati's genealogy and early years. All of that—questions, fears, even the pain in my stomach—vanished as soon as I saw Nati's mother.

She was wearing a tan jacket and a blue sweater. Her sister, Nati's aunt, was wearing a brown suit. Neither woman would have looked out of place in any American city. I'm sorry to say that I must have thought that wouldn't be the case, since their very ordinariness threw me. We got out of the car and Nati's mother hugged him, though he seemed a bit shy. It occurred to me that this moment was going to be the last time I would ever again not be responsible for Nati, the last time he would not fully be my own child. And all of the questions I was prepared to ask, about Nati's childhood illnesses, his father's background, his upbringing, all of those things, simply ceased to exist for me. I felt an understanding settling inside me. I wasn't there to gather information, or to learn anything. I wasn't even there for Nati, not as his guardian or father. I was there to watch a mother say good-bye to her son and there simply wasn't room for anything else.

Mostly what I remember from that day were her eyes. They were red from tears, yellowed from illness. They were the saddest eyes I've ever seen. Nati sat on his mother's lap and she stroked his head. After a while, I asked Sara to ask Nati's mother if she'd mind if I took some photos for Nati to have later. She agreed. I took the pictures. *These are photos your son will look at after you're gone*, I thought to myself. *These are his memories of you for when he lives far away from you, far away from here.* I felt as if I were doing something cold and cruel. The conversation was all in Amharic, though I sensed not much was being said, not in words, anyway. I watched as Nati's mother said good-bye to her son, knowing that she couldn't take care of him, knowing that this impossible act was the best she could now do. She held on to him, whispering into his ear, as though she could imprint a memory of herself into his consciousness through sheer whispered will.

I'd brought pictures of Mary, our home, of Clay and Grace. I took them out and had Sara translate as I showed the pictures around. I tried to find the perfect words, though everything I said was being translated. I avoided saying that Clay was "my son," not wanting her to think that I didn't consider Nati to be the same as a son, and yet not wanting her to think that I did, either. "This is Clay; he'll be Nati's brother," I said.

"This is Gracie." "This is where Nati will go to school." "This is my home." Nati, on the other hand, was under no such constraints. He and I had looked at all of the pictures; we'd used them as flash cards in our hotel room together so that he could learn the names and faces of his new family.

"American mom!" he shouted out when we came to a photo of Mary. "Brother Clay! Sister Grace. Nati house!"

I cringed and tried to smile.

After a half hour, Nati's aunt, who seemed almost to be in charge, began indicating it was time to leave. A moment later, she turned to Sara and spoke. Sara then turned to me and said that both Nati's mother and his aunt were wondering if I would come back the next day so that other family members could come and say good-bye. I agreed, of course, but knew that somewhere my own parents were laughing. After years of dodging bar mitzvahs, weddings, and assorted family gatherings, I was now trapped into going to back-to-back family reunions.

That night I spoke to Mary and told her about meeting Nati's mother. It had gone well, I thought. It was hard, but not nearly overwhelming, as I'd feared. Nati, too, seemed all right. He and I played a few games together in our hotel room, had some dinner, and watched TV, and then I put him to bed, as was our routine. All was well.

The next day, we arrived at the same restaurant but were met by a much larger group. There was Nati's aunt, wearing the same brown suit she'd worn the day before. There were two friends of Nati's mother, there to give support. One of Nati's cousins, about eighteen years old, sat to one side, where he spoke little. An older woman, Nati's grandmother, dressed in traditional Ethiopian clothing, sat at the end of the table, a blue scarf on her head. A woman in her early twenties told me in perfect English that she was Nati's cousin. Another cousin was introduced. I sat down, consciously trying to slip into the background, not that I was likely to go unnoticed anywhere in Ethiopia. I took more pictures and listened as they all chatted. I was offered food and drinks, but passed. My driver cheerfully informed the group that I had been quite sick and was, for that reason, unable to eat with them, and everyone there happily laughed at me. Nati was patient and sat on his mother's lap as she fed him spoonfuls of a drink. Mostly he looked bored, the way kids do when they're stuck at a table filled with nothing but grown-ups.

I sat next to Nati's cousin and was able to quietly ask a few questions. She told me the only things I was ever to learn about Nati's father, a tiny few facts about who he was and what he'd done. Nati's cousin wasn't especially emotional as she told me about my new son's father, not even when describing how he died thinking of his son, calling his name. She was a gentle woman and kind, but she was not dramatic; she did not cry or hesitate in finding her words.

Nati sat on his grandmother's lap. He had stayed for a time with his grandmother, just prior to going to the orphanage, and I learned later that his memories of his grandmother were good and that he'd been happy with her. Adults began passing him around. I found out that Nati thought of his male teenage cousin, who had said next to nothing, as his "brother," and I wondered if perhaps that was true, if perhaps he was Nati's brother and I simply wasn't being told the truth. It didn't matter in the least.

Nati was back, after a while, with his mother. Her eyes grew redder. She and I had spoken very little. I asked Nati's female cousin to translate for me, and then drew a bit closer to Nati's mother. My wife, I told her, would want me to say that we would take good care of her son. That he would have wonderful opportunities with us, a great school, a nice home, the chance to become whatever he wanted to be as he grew older. I said that we would love him and care for him. She nodded, but the words all seemed like dust coming out of my mouth. All of those things, the chance to have her son get a decent education, the hope that he would grow up in a prosperous and safe country, that his needs and wants would all be met, they were all not of that moment. This woman, with her tired, pained eyes, had decided long ago to give up her son, so that he could be part of a family and have all of those things after she was gone, but now, none of them mattered to her at all, not in any real way. She was saying good-bye, and though I was the one Nati would be leaving with, I was, for that moment, a distraction and nothing else.

When it came time to leave, Nati's mother didn't sob, but her eyes filled with tears and her face grew pained. Nati and I got into our car and I told him to wave to his family. They stood there in the dirt parking lot of a restaurant in Addis Ababa and watched us go.

It would be unforgivably shallow if I were to trivialize Nati's mother's sacrifice and pain by comparing it to any struggle I go through in my comfortable life in the U.S. But it would be just as unforgivable if I didn't do all that I could to use her sacrifice and pain to make myself a better father to her son.

The woman who handed me her child, the bravest woman I will ever meet, was doing something that ran counter to the strongest instinct any parent ever has: *to hold on*. We may have lightly dismissed our own parents' attempts to be in charge of us, but we promise ourselves we're different. Our children will be different. We know best. We have to be in charge.

And yet there I was with a woman who somehow had found the strength to let go. She was doing what was best for her son at the greatest personal cost any parent could ever imagine. She was letting go of him because if she didn't let go, then and there, she knew he might not be taken care of later on. And so she let go.

And in doing so, she taught me how I would have to let go too. It's horrible to say that, but I was there. I watched, and in watching the single most awful thing I've ever seen, a mother saying good-bye to her son, to my son, I found out how I could discover the grace to make the much less wrenching but still difficult daily surrenders I'd have to make.

It bears repeating. Nothing I have ever had to do could, in

any way, compare to what Nati's mother went through giving up her son. I would have to be criminally insensitive not to be aware of that fact or to ever let it stray far from my thoughts. But it is also true that the intense love we feel as parents for our children often leaves us in a state of anxiety and panic, even over things that in retrospect are far from life and death.

Looking back, seeing that moment in my mind's eye, I know what Nati's mother was doing with her son. She was setting the course for his life knowing that she would not be able to dictate each of the thousands of turns that would make up that course. Paradoxically, in those last moments with him, Nati's mother was both letting go of her son and doing all she could to guide his future. She was placing her faith in the idea that her sacrifice would help mold her son's future far more than anything else ever could. She was resigning herself to the heartbreaking fact that only by giving up any chance of controlling any of the thousands of small moments to come could she manage to influence each and every one of those moments. She was implanting herself onto Nati's heart and brain and soul. She was helping to create his character and trusting that the character she was creating would in turn help create his destiny. She would not have the last word on his daily life, but she would have the far more important first words, the ones that would set the tone for everything to come.

And that, I know now, is all any parent can ever do.

Starting the conversation while leaving my children with

the last word is the third way, the one between a thousand arguments with your kids and leaving them entirely to their own devices. I have grown to have faith in the first words, and that has let me give up needing to have the last ones.

I had already learned some of the limits of my own power. The great paradox for me is that while nothing on earth makes me want to hold on, to be in control, and to micromanage quite as much as raising my children, it is just as true that nothing on earth thwarts my attempts to control and micromanage quite as much as raising my children.

One day I read a magazine article and a year later I had a five-year-old son who didn't speak English, whose mother had given him to me with love and trust, and whom I did not know. I had found throughout the process of adopting Nati, and most especially as I left Ethiopia with him, that I was not in charge of much of anything. As I think about my teenage children now, all three of them, I see that while that principle was clearer in Nati's case than it sometimes was with Grace and Clay, it was no less true of them.

I suppose first I should get rid of the silly objections, the paper tigers it would be so easy to place between me and a sane life. For example, if I'm not in charge, does that mean the kids make themselves candy bars for dinner while I lounge around in my robe watching TV? Don't be ridiculous, that's only on Father's Day. I feed my kids nutritious food because that's part of being their parent. Am I saying that I don't care who my daughter hangs out with? Not at all. I casually mention to my daughter that all boys are bad each and every day, because I'm her father and that's my job (plus, it's sort of fun). What I don't do is believe that I am in charge of their futures. I want them to do their homework and when called upon, I'm willing to get in my car and drive at night to the office-supply store to buy the red highlighting marker they forgot to tell me they needed until the very last day, because that's what parents do, but I no longer live my life as if the completion of any one homework assignment will dictate all of my child's future happiness. I have seen too much, in Ethiopia and for a long time afterward here in my home, that has taught me the simple, humbling truths that guide me every day.

I have influence, but not control. And influence is all I really want, need, and deserve.

I am not always grateful for that knowledge. There are times when it would be nice to live my life as if I had total control over what happens to me and the people I love. It would be nice sometimes to forget about Nati's mother and how she looked as she, with more love than I could imagine, gave her son to me to raise and to care for. It would be nice to believe that I am the master of my children's destinies, that I know what is best for them and that I am capable of delivering it to them.

But since I know that is not true, I am left to decide how best to live my life in the world I must live it in. I can accept and even embrace the fact that so much of what is truly amazing and remarkable in the world happens without anyone asking my permission for it to occur. I know too that my kids will have to make their own decisions, thousands of them, even before I think they're ready to do just that (and I know that for a fact, since my mother still seems pretty sure I'm not ready to make all my own decisions yet).

And so I get to choose. Will I try to have the last word or the first? Will I try to tell my kids how they should keep their rooms, who they should be with, what colleges they should apply to, and what to wear to school, knowing that they will rebel and that my life and theirs will be spent smashing our heads together not in spite of how much I love them, but because of how much I love them? Or will I give all that up and concentrate only on setting the tone, through my words, actions, and daily behavior, showing them by how I treat them and the people around me what I value and what I consider meaningful?

Seeing Nati's mother on that day in Ethiopia taught me that I could trust that if I behaved with enough love and decency in front of my children, I could allow myself to accept that I could not control their every moment.

And so maybe what's changed for me isn't so much what I do, but how I do it.

Think of it as a tale of two sinks. There are dirty dishes in the sink and your kid is supposed to have done them. I know, it's hard to imagine that kind of scenario, but work with me for a second here.

If I am in charge of my child's future and the molder of

his or her destiny, the dirty sink is a problem. It's a problem because I know, deep within my soul, that my child is going to grow up to be undisciplined. He is going to be selfish and not care about other people. And he's going to be a terrible slob. In the short amount of time it takes me to go from looking at the sink to shouting at my kids, I've done all the mental gymnastics necessary to see a future in which my dirty, sloppy child is living alone (who would marry such a selfish slob?) in squalor with hordes of bugs swarming around him because food has piled up everywhere in his apartment. He's unemployed because he's too irresponsible to even remember to wash dirty silverware, and so it won't be long before he's back living in my house, cluttering up my sink. Is it any wonder parents lose their tempers?

Now, let's take a look at a different sink, or rather, the same sink . . . differently. Yeah, the dishes are there. But that's all that's in the sink—dirty dishes. Not the revolting evidence of a future failure. Dirty dishes. I see them and accept that I'm not in charge of what happens to my kids twenty years from now. I know that my children have seen me clean our kitchen sink so that my wife—who, after all, is the one in the family who has to put on decent clothes and go to work every day in an office—won't have to do that chore herself.

Maybe they'll change on their own. Maybe they'll always be sloppy. Maybe a job will come in some unexpected way and maybe that job will pay them enough to hire someone to come and do their dishes. Maybe they'll marry someone who's smart, funny, and kind and who's drawn to them because of their casual, relaxed approach to hygiene.

And then again, maybe it's just a sink filled with dishes. What then?

If my kids seem busy with homework, I do the dishes. If they just forgot, I remind them. If they're being selfish and, you know . . . *childish*, I try not to lose my mind over it. Children, after all, do tend to be childish, and then they tend to grow out of it, all on their own. I let go of my fears about what will happen if I don't nag, because they're going to grow out of being children and this is my life too. And I refuse to spend too much of it panicked about things I can't control. And yes, sometimes that includes my sink. All I can do, even when it comes to something as trivial as a dirty sink, is show them what I value and why I value it. I value kindness. I value treating other people with respect and dignity. I value not having a swarm of flies hovering over a sink filled with dirty dishes. I live those values. Sometimes I do that by being kind enough to help my kids with their dishes when they have a lot of homework. Other times I live those values by telling them I'm really busy and asking them to do a bit extra so I can get other stuff done. Sometimes it's enough that they simply see me doing things for their mom so she won't have to. Most of all, every now and again, I just clean the damn dishes without worrying about what that sink means for the course of their lives.

Every parent who's ever yelled at a child for not doing a

chore has muttered, "It would be easier to do this myself," and you know what, sometimes that's true. And if the only reason you're not doing "it," whatever it happens to be at that moment, is because you think nagging your children will guarantee that they will become responsible job-holding adults ten or twenty years from now . . . uh, maybe that's something you want to really rethink. I didn't start doing dishes when I moved into my first apartment because my mother had nagged me about "responsibility" for eighteen years. I did the dishes when I moved out because I was living alone and I needed a fork. I spent years begging Clay not to leave his wet towels on his floor. Then, one day, I just gave up. You know what happened? He got older. Old enough to want girls to come over. When he asked me why his room smelled musty sometimes, I calmly told him that wet towels on carpet creates a bad smell. Now he picks up his towels. Think I could have spared myself all that time demanding he change, since he was going to change anyway? Isn't that the question parents should ask themselves?

And if your child doesn't change? What happens if they stay sloppy and let the dishes pile up in the sink once they're in their twenties and thirties and beyond? What then? Well, uh, nothing. I have friends who are neat and I have friends who are not. Sometimes the neat ones fail in their professional and personal endeavors and sometimes they succeed. Same with the sloppy ones. The time that their parents spent trying to make the sloppy kids neater had absolutely no effect on the

*Grace and Clay meet Nati for the first time in the airport.*

lives they led. None. Well, except of course, those parents did succeed in making everyone involved, including themselves, miserable. So, there was that.

Are you really sure you want to give up decades of your life losing your peace of mind badgering your kids because you're afraid of what will happen if you don't? I have my kids take out the garbage sometimes because it makes my life easier. I put their dishes in the dishwasher sometimes because that also makes my life easier. Sometimes my kids do a lot around the house; other times, not so much. At no time, however, do I feel that berating and hassling my children to put away their shoes will force them into becoming compassionate, responsible, hardworking adults. I do not have that kind of control over my children's destinies. I am not that powerful and because I now know that I am not that powerful, I no longer waste my time trying to control what can not be controlled. I hope my actions and attitudes will influence my kids, but that's it. Instead of screaming, I simply try to live my life in a way that shows them what I hope they will be.

Nati is my son. I have three children. That they exist in my life seems miraculous to me still. And if I believe, as I truly do, that I am not driving a car but am rather, more or less, a passenger on a train whose tracks have already been laid out for me, what's next is for me to try to figure out how best to relax and enjoy the ride.

# WORRYING DOESN'T HELP WHEN YOU DON'T KNOW HOW TO WORRY

*How Knowing Only Four Words*

*of My Son's Language Taught Me*

*to Give Up Being Afraid*

T WOULD BE EASIER IF WE WEREN'T SO MUCH SMARTER THAN them. It would be so much easier if our fears and concerns were wrong.

Really, it would. You would think that knowing so much would make life better for us, but it just doesn't work that way. We can see so much further than our kids can, and all that knowledge about the future does nothing but make us miserable. Because we know what they should be worried about, we worry for them. We know how much better their lives would be if only they would, well, let's see . . . uh, actually, it's a pretty long list.

We know our kids' lives would be better if only they would: study harder, take school more seriously, let us pick their friends, be more responsible, not wear that skirt, cut their hair, study without making themselves quite so crazy, eat more vegetables, write thank-you notes, stand up straighter, get a firmer handshake, do their homework before they watch TV, text less, play an instrument, stick with a sport, learn to be more responsible by doing their chores, and most of all, pay attention to what we're saying. Because we know what's best and we know what to be afraid will happen if they don't follow our advice. Which would be fine, if only our kids would listen and do exactly what we think they should do.

They don't, though. Which is hard on us, because we

also know what will happen if our kids *don't* do all the things we know they should do. We know if they don't learn to shake hands firmly they won't impress people enough to get good jobs. We know if they don't text less they won't get into good schools, and we know without any question that their boyfriends and girlfriends are going to cause them nothing but misery.

We know exactly what our children should and should not do so that they can live happy and fulfilling lives, which makes the fact that we tend to be overwhelmed, nervous wrecks prone to snapping at our children sort of odd. You might even understand how our kids don't believe us when we tell them we know what they should do to be happy given that we seem so very unhappy while we're trying to help them. You might even wonder if everything we know about how the people closest to us should be living their lives is true—if, that is, you had enough time to think about it. Which we don't.

We know better, and because we know better, we're sort of miserable. And so we're stuck. We try to force them into doing what we know will help them and then we're locked into arguments and stuck living with sullen kids who should thank us for helping them, but never do. Ever.

And we can't stop ourselves from micromanaging be-cause, well, because we know best. Life can seem like a mine-field, with all sorts of hidden booby traps waiting to strike. But we're older and smarter and so we have the map of the minefield, and of course we want to share that information.

The thought of letting our kids wander around this confusing and dangerous world without our constant help is terrifying, and so we seem condemned to fight them if only so we can protect them from all the stuff we're so afraid will happen if we don't take charge. Because we have the map, we know what our kids should be afraid of. We can see around corners and catch the monsters that are lurking just out of sight. Study harder, stand up straighter, do as we say, or you'll be doomed. We know so much, but somehow every piece of knowledge we think we have about the world winds up being another brick on our chest that stops us from breathing.

Me, I'm lucky. I had a way of keeping score when it came to all the things I thought I knew. By the time Nati had been home for only a little while, I had a pretty good idea of just what kind of a track record I had in terms of knowing what to fear. And the very sad, very clear truth is that my map of that minefield turned out not to be all that useful after all.

See, when Nati first came home, I had a few things I knew I should be worried about. For example, there was the whole problem with the four words.

Because I'd foolishly chosen to study Spanish in high school instead of the Ethiopian language of Amharic, when Nati came to America, I knew exactly four of the words he knew. Those four words were:

*shent*

*bakka*

*kaka*

*ishi*

Four words. Really only three words, since one of them means the same in English as it does in Amharic.

The fact that I knew only four words of Nati's language worried me. That Nati didn't speak English at all was downright terrifying. Plus, there was that other thing.

True, on the ride home from the airport, after our long flight from Ethiopia, he quietly began singing "Twinkle, Twinkle, Little Star" to himself in the backseat of our car. It was one of the cutest things I've ever seen, Nati gently kicking his leg back and forth, singing almost to himself as he stared out at a city with more buildings and lights than he'd ever seen in his life. He'd been taught the song at the orphanage, but sadly he didn't have a clue what any of the words he was singing actually meant.

Not *twinkle*.

Not *little*.

Not *star*.

So no real conversation starters there.

Sometimes, before Nati came to America, people reminded me to be worried about the fact that my new son and I wouldn't be able to communicate. Friends would say things like, "You must be really worried about his not speaking English," or, "If I were you, I'd be so worried about not being able to talk to him." Other times people would try to be helpful by asking, "Have you given any thought to how you'll talk to him? He's not going to speak English, you know." So we worried.

A better, smarter man might have learned more of his new son's native tongue, but those four words were all I managed. Nati, of course, spoke less of my language than I did of his. Before Nati arrived, Mary and I worried a lot. There seemed to be no way that we'd find our way around the problem of spending every waking minute with a five-year-old boy who wouldn't be able to talk to us. Mary and I did one day go to an Ethiopian restaurant that wasn't far from us, where we asked around to find someone who might do the occasional bit of translation. There we met Shewaye, a nice woman who agreed to come by for two hours a week to translate. It was only now and then, but it was useful, particularly when she told us during Nati's second week with us that he liked his new brother and sister very much, that he couldn't believe how many toys there were in America, and that he was having a wee bit of trouble sleeping at night because he was concerned that there might be hyenas in the tree by his bedroom window. Through Shewaye, we assured Nati that California was pretty well hyena-free, which seemed to help a bit.

But Shewaye was dropping by only now and then at that point. Which meant that there was a whole lot of time when Nati and I simply didn't speak the same language. Which was easy to worry about.

My worry that Nati didn't speak any English wasn't entirely irrational. A really good thing to worry about is never really *entirely* irrational. After all, if you worry that your child is going to be abducted by aliens, you're crazy. If you worry that your child's inherited lack of math skills will ultimately derail their chances of getting into a really great college, then you're just being proactive, even if your child happens to be six years old. We were living with and raising a child who didn't speak English. A small bit of concern was not totally without merit.

Did I have trouble communicating with Nati? Yes. There's no denying that we had our moments. There was the day when Nati had been home with us for just a couple of weeks and he and I went out to run errands, getting things ready for my daughter's sixth birthday. It was difficult to explain to Nati that Gracie was going to be getting a lot of gifts not because I liked her best but only because her birthday was coming up and that he, too, would get plenty of presents when his birthday came around in October. Then again, both of my already-fluent-in-English children had the same problems with watching their biological sibling get birthday gifts in the past, so I tended to think that the issue had a lot more to do with Nati being five than with anything related to his grasp of language.

The errands went smoothly until Nati began saying *"mesa."* It had been a few weeks, so I'd learned that in Amharic, *mesa* translates to "lunch," but Nati had also learned a few things, like the fact that I am very bad with languages.

From the second when I began ignorantly offering Nati "lunch" for breakfast, lunch, and dinner, he had more or less agreed to say *"mesa"* whenever he wanted food of any kind.

I pulled the car over and slowly and loudly asked, "WHAT . . . NATI . . . EAT . . . *MESA?*" (I might as well make a confession here. You know how some really stupid people try to communicate with foreigners who don't speak their language by shouting and speaking slowly? Like, they might say, "WHHHHAAAT'S YOOOOUUURRR NAAAMMMEEE?" as if somehow that would make someone from France understand English? Yeah. That was me. Not proud of it, but speaking slowly and loudly to Nati was what I did instead of studying Amharic. Perhaps this would be a good moment to point out that panic has rarely produced sound and useful solutions in my life.)

So when I asked him, "WHAT . . . NATI . . . EAT . . . *MESA?*" I felt confident I'd get a reply I could understand. Which is why when Nati said *"pinlo,"* I made what I felt fairly sure we both thought of as the "I'm sorry Daddy's so stupid but I have no idea what you're saying" face. Nati repeated the word, which I decided might be *pinta, menta,* or *fenta.* I called Mary at work, held the phone up to Nati, and got him to repeat his lunch order. Mary, a college graduate and managing director at her firm, suggested Nati was saying "Mentos," and that I should go to a candy store and buy him some of those oddly popular mints. I declined, because it now seemed to me that Nati was saying "pinto," and thus wanted a plateful of beans. A final call to my sister, Jeanine, after the fact, raised yet another possibility. Nati, Jeanine felt, was really asking for "pimentos," though when I pointed out that seemed unlikely, she did admit he probably wanted the whole olive and not just that red thing they stuff in the middle.

In the end, I just took Nati to a place I wanted to go to, ordered him French fries, and a Mickey Mouse–shaped pancake, and let him dig in. Later, Shewaye told me Nati was actually asking for *misto*, an Ethiopian stew that mixes lamb and beef.

Still, we ate. Really, at some point, solutions just wound up presenting themselves, as solutions usually do. Because there sometimes seem to be only two kinds of problems. There are the problems I'm afraid I'll have in the future, which are impossible to solve. (Which is not surprising. It's very hard to solve something that hasn't happened yet.) And then there are the problems I actually have. Those problems, the ones that actually exist, often work themselves out without much help at all.

Nati, for example, needed chest X-rays as part of some routine physical exams when he'd only been here a short while. Because he was beginning to learn some English, I tried to make sure he knew that unlike an earlier visit, there would be "no shot for Nati." I acted out what a "shot for Nati" would look like and then I shook my head over and over and said, "No, no, no."

Pretty subtle, but yeah, he got it.

I kept repeating that magic phrase, "no shot for Nati," and while we sat in the waiting room, Nati began to joke, saying, "No shot Nati, shot Mom." I'd then say, "No shot Mom, shot Dad," and so on till we'd pretty much vaccinated the entire family and all of our pets. Finally, a guy in a lab coat called our name and motioned us to follow him, at which point Nati lost all faith in me. His eyes grew very large; he started chewing on his thumbnail and all in all made it clear that he knew this "no shot Nati" stuff was all a trick. I did my best to calm him, repeating the phrase "no shot Nati" over and over. We went into the X-ray room, and the guy in the lab coat had me stand in a separate part of the room out of range of the machine and then told Nati where to stand.

"I'm sorry, he doesn't speak English," I said.

The lab guy nodded and then told Nati how important it was that he didn't move at all.

I explained again that my son didn't speak English, then looked at Nati and said "no shot" a few more times. Then I began moving my arms around like an octopus undergoing an electric shock treatment. "Look, Nati," I said. "Daddy move. Move." I did this until (a) the guy in the lab coat began looking alarmed and (b) Nati began to understand what the word *move* meant. I then stood very still and said, "No move," and then, "Nati no move." Nati laughed and then said, "No move." The lab coat guy went to take a picture.

Nati moved. Because he wanted to, you know, avoid getting a shot.

I ran back in to do the whole octopus dance thing again. Between my spasms and Nati's panicked attempts to dodge a shot that he wasn't going to get, we were at a bit of an impasse.

After that, I'm pretty sure God himself decided enough was enough.

I don't know where she'd been hiding, I certainly hadn't seen her, but out of nowhere, a woman came rushing into the room and asked, "Does he speak Amharic?"

It's not a question I was used to getting asked.

I scooped my jaw back up from the floor and nodded, and the lab coat guy's assistant, who had moved here from Ethiopia some time ago, told Nati what was going on. Simple as 1-2-3, or, as my son would have put it then, *"ahnd-huleutt-sost."*

Of course, when people asked how I communicated with Nati, they were really just asking me how we had talked about the importance of brushing your teeth, or how we'd communicated to him that we'd rather he flushed the toilet each and every time after he'd finished using it and not just now and then. In the end, though, those things can be taken care of by speaking loudly and slowly. What made communicating hard with Nati wasn't the language gap at all; it was the same thing that can make it hard to talk to any of my three kids to this day: fear.

When I am frightened about my children and their futures, I become like a man who's wearing binoculars and doesn't know it. Small things seem huge to me and I act in a way that's perfectly appropriate to me based on what I'm seeing (as opposed to how I might act based on, you know, what's actually happening). So when Nati did something as normal and unexciting as sticking his tongue out at Gracie, we'd panic and wonder if maybe he'd been walking around the house for two weeks muttering horrible things to himself about women and that he'd never be able to form attachments with Mary or any other women because of what he'd gone through leaving Africa. We worried that maybe Grace would unconsciously start to believe that being treated badly by men was in some way okay. We worried about lifelong patterns developing in Nati and Grace, about problems that would take years of struggle to overcome and change.

Yeah. He was five. Five-year-olds sometimes stick their tongues out at their sisters. You know what a really good solution for that problem is? Shrugging. Shrugging would have covered that whole problem. But fear makes every problem bigger. And, of course, every normal situation that I'd gone through before Nati came along was certainly made more stark by the language barrier and just plain weirdness of so much of our lives. Yes, not being able to communicate with Nati could sometimes drive us crazy, but then, we were so close to crazy we could have walked there ourselves anyway.

The thing was, when we weren't panicked, we could communicate just fine. When we were panicked, all the words in the world couldn't help us say a thing. Which, I've noticed, tends to be true for me in my relationships with pretty much everyone I know.

Besides, I did know those few words.

The most important one was *shent*, which means "pee."

Being afraid that my son and I spoke different languages had seemed very reasonable. (All of my fears always seem very reasonable. That's how fears are. They don't need to storm the gates of my mind like a barbarian horde sacking ancient Rome. Instead, they knock. Gently and quietly my fears knock on the doors of my brain to tell me they've come up with some useful information. Nati doesn't speak English. He probably is saying that he hates his sister. What are you going to do about it? Really, you ought to do something before she realizes that he doesn't respect women and she starts dating inappropriate men when she's older. See? Perfectly reasonable. At least to me, around three thirty in the morning when I can't sleep.) And yet there's a certain limit to how much you can discuss with any five-year-old boy, and once you know the word for "pee" you're going to be more set for conversation than you might think.

"Nati *shent?*" I'd ask five or six times an hour, both to see if he needed to pee and, more important, to make conversation while we ate. When Nati did need to *shent,* I'd take him to a bathroom. I'd taught him to lift the seat to pee, then to flush the toilet, and finally, as a favor to his future wife, to put the seat back down after he'd peed. Unable to believe he'd be expected to do all of that each and every time he went to the bathroom, Nati, in a concession to my limited vocabulary, would ask, *"shent* up?" as he lifted the seat, *"shent* fleeesh?" as he flushed the toilet, and finally, *"shent* down?" as he put the seat down. *Shent* was not the only bathroom-related word I learned, though as it happens the Amharic word for, well, caca, is, as luck would have it, *kaka*, which sort of felt like cheating.

Unlike the rather childish-sounding *kaka*, the word *shent* proved to be quite popular with both of my English-speaking children. Thus it was far from unusual to hear my eight-year-old, blond-haired son say, "I've got to go *shent*, Dad"; to hear my wife say, "Clay, hurry up and *shent* so we can leave"; or even to hear my daughter say, "Daddy, Nati missed the toilet and *shent*ed on the floor again." Indeed, when Nati had been in America for a few months, parents of Nati's classmates often were confused when their sons and daughters announced that they'd be just another minute, since they had to *shent* before leaving for school.

*Ishi* was even more useful.

*Ishi* means "okay." But not just "okay" as in, "I agree"; after all, I already could communicate a yes by nodding my head and smiling a lot. "Okay" as in "yes" is just the beginning of all that can be expressed by saying *ishi*. *Ishi* also means "okay, okay," as in, "Stop talking and get in the car, we're late."

*Ishi* can be a way of indicating concern when a child falls: "*Ishi?*" It can, if said with the proper tone, even be used to comfort a child who feels lost and alone because he is thousands of miles away from his home, his friends, and what's left of his family. "*Ishi?*"

Like the word *shent*, the word *ishi* proved to be very popular with the English-speaking members of my family. When Nati took a toy that Gracie thought of as "special," she tried to give him a different toy in its place. "*Ishi?* Nati, *ishi?*" she asked as she held out the substitute toy. My wife and I both found ourselves telling Clay and Grace, "*Ishi, ishi . . .*" when they were demanding something or other, and on more than one occasion I tried to get my English-speaking dogs to stop barking by saying "*Ishi!*" We told our children they could have candy at the movies like we'd promised ten thousand times before by saying "*Ishi, ishi*"; we settled arguments by saying "*Ishi*" to one and all; we have even healed boo-boos with an "*Ishi*" and a kiss. Truly, this is one remarkable word.

Even more useful than *ishi*, however, was another word, one that no parent should be without regardless of what language their child speaks. That word is *bakka*, which is Amharic for "Knock it off!" or, if you prefer, "Enough!" or, depending on occasion, "Give it a rest before Daddy starts weeping uncontrollably." *Bakka*, which rhymes with one of the few other Amharic words I knew, can be spoken to children and pets of all nationalities. It can be spoken in anger, frustration, resignation, and, most of all, in disbelief. Your daughter won't stop texting during dinner? Your son won't stop asking for candy before, or perhaps instead of, dinner? Your kid wants to see if he can Rollerblade down your staircase? Bring on the *bakka*, and plenty of it.

We'd worried and worried, but through a combination of miracles or serendipity or whatever else you prefer to call the sudden appearance of an Amharic-speaking X-ray technician, and my four words of Amharic, we managed. I don't know how much time I'd wasted wondering how we'd deal with that huge crisis that never really occurred, but in the end it was all pretty *ishi*.

Still, there was that other thing.

The other thing was a source of great concern for us and everyone we spoke with. Some people brought it up without hesitation. Others were a bit more cautious. But the other thing seemed to be on everyone's mind.

People had all sorts of ways of bringing it up. "Are you worried about him not connecting to you because you're white?" was a pretty typical approach. We also got a few people who helpfully asked, "Are you nervous about raising a child who's so visually different from the rest of you?" In the end, my favorite version of the question was a bit more direct. All three kids and I were standing waiting to pay for some groceries when the guy working the register asked if they were all mine. I said yes and after a long thoughtful pause, he turned toward Nati and said in total sincerity and with a clear desire to help, "You know he's black, right?"

Nati was, is, and forever shall be black. Mary, Clay, Grace, and I . . . are not. And so we worried. Who wouldn't? We worried that he would resent us, we worried that he would always feel different from us. We worried that we weren't worried enough about something that could be so worth worrying about. We worried that there would be a mysterious gulf that would always separate us from our new child. We worried that he would never connect with us. We worried about bullies and bigots and how we could best create a sensitive multicultural family that would appropriately embrace our differences while still emphasizing our commonalities.

And now, years later, let me just say one thing about all of that.

Meh. It's fine. Thanks for asking.

Does it sound like I'm turning the complicated and potentially explosive topic of having a mixed-race family into something worthy of no more than an eye roll? Yup, guilty.

I can't say that the fact that Nati is a young black man being raised by a white mother and father won't be a problem for him some day. He is now sixteen years old and yes, there are times when I know it's an issue for him.

And yet . . . meh.

As in, so far, so good.

True, early on, when we flew to New York for my niece's bat mitzvah, one of my uncles, not one of the brighter ones, took Nati aside and asked him, "So, are you going to grow up to play basketball in the NBA?" In fact, Nati used to get asked that one a lot. Sometimes, for some funny reason, it happened even when he was wearing a football jersey. There are just some people who look at him and for some reason assume he's a basketball guy. Generally, those same people would walk up to Clay, shake his hand, and say, "Nice to meet you, Clay," and then turn to Nati and say, "Nati! Give me a high five," as if they and Nati had just been cast in the remake of *Shaft*.

Once, Mary and I took all three of our kids to dinner one night after Nati had been here about three months. A woman holding a baby walked up to our table, stood in front of us, and stared for about thirty seconds. Thirty seconds doesn't sound like much, but it's a pretty long time to have a strange woman stand in front of your table watching you eat. After Mary and I started staring back, she finally wandered away.

But, honestly, the whole multicultural-family/sensitivity/embracing-the-differences thing hasn't really been much of an issue. Nati has been relearning Amharic, the language he came to America knowing. He might stick with it too. Then again, he might not. He's a teenager. Stuff changes. As a family, we eat Ethiopian food now and again. When he wants a raise in his allowance and I say no, Nati will, without fail, look at me and say, "Really, Dad? You know I'm from Africa, right?" And when I say no when he wants me to buy him something, whether it's new clothes, a car, or a controlling interest in a Fortune 500 company, Nati will almost always reply, "Really? Is it because I'm black?" to which I always reply, "No, it's because you're Jewish."

Meh.

An issue we'd been utterly confounded by has so far turned out to be worth nothing more than a giant shrug and a *meh*. Once, years ago, I played a song in the car by the Dixie Chicks, and Nati bent over and began howling until I played something by Kanye West, but other than that, meh. Nati is still black, and Mary, Clay, Grace, and I are still not. Sometimes that has been an issue; sometimes it has not. It's never been that big a deal.

Look, I don't want to imply that race isn't important. It is. Nor am I dumb enough to say that Nati won't be affected by the fact that he so clearly looks different from the rest of his family. We have talked frankly to him about how different people will perceive him sometimes, and those conversations are painful in different ways to Nati and Mary and me. It's a complicated and, at times, cruel world. I get that. That will all affect him.

That Nati is the only black person in his family does certainly mean something and will, without question, affect him in a myriad of ways. I have had to awkwardly ask friends of mine who are black if I was right to think that maybe I should be preparing Nati for a world in which some authority figures, from police officers to store owners to school administrators, might treat him as someone to watch warily based on nothing other than his skin color, and I have felt horribly saddened as those men rushed to assure me that yes, that conversation was one I had to have with my son. That Nati is a young black man being raised by white parents is important and significant and something he will always carry as part of who he is, for better and for worse.

I know that race factors into every part of our lives. I see that a good deal more clearly now than I ever did before.

But—

One of the most remarkable moments of my time in Ethiopia picking up Nati took place in the small room that functioned as a classroom. I was speaking, as best I could, to a group of kids who had been adopted but, owing to the vast amount of paperwork involved in international adoptions, had not yet been cleared to go home with their new families. There was a map in the room and one by one the kids told me where they were going to be living. A tall boy, older than Nati, told me that his new family lived in a place called Minnesota. I smiled and pretended to shiver. "Cold," I said. "You'll go skiing in winter." I pantomimed skiing as best I could, and they all laughed. A girl told me she would be moving to Georgia, and I tried to tell her about how hot it got there in the summer. Another child would be living in New York City and, as best I could, I described tall, tall buildings, bigger than any she'd ever seen in her life.

Each of those children was going to be plucked almost at random from the place they'd always known so they could be raised in circumstances totally alien to them. Where they lived, how many brothers and sisters they were about to have, what their new parents did for a living: All of those things were going to have an effect on them. I have never been so consciously aware of what words like *destiny* and *fate* meant. Obviously, being a part of a family he doesn't physically resemble will have an effect on Nati, just as being adopted by a family in Utah instead of Miami would affect any of the kids I was with in that schoolroom that day. But being affected by something is what life is about. It's how we grow, form, and evolve. Nati is affected by issues of race. But all of the fear and well-meaning anxiety I had about race, about how it would affect Nati and Clay and Grace . . . meh. As in, it comes up but not nearly as often as we talk about what we're having for dinner.

So yeah, maybe I could have worried less about that one. Or, you know, not at all.

The third and final thing we worried about the most before Nati came home with me wasn't about Nati at all. It was about Clay. And again, in that worry, we were way off.

As a now-mature teenager, Clay is consistent and loyal. As a seven-year-old who was about to meet his five-year-old brother from Africa for the first time, he was more rigid and inflexible than a brick. He liked what he liked, and change was not what he liked. Good change, bad change, he was against it.

Take, for instance, breakfast. When Clay was three, I found some instant oatmeal with "dinosaur eggs," which, I assume, hope, and pray, are actually just lumps of sugar. I gave Clay that instant oatmeal for breakfast and he liked it. So he had it the next day. Clay is eighteen as I write this and he had that same brand of oatmeal for breakfast this morning. And yes, in case you're wondering, every day in between as well. I buy it online now in bulk, sixteen or twenty boxes at a time because it's cheaper that way.

And so when we announced plans to create an actual dinosaur-sized change in our children's lives, friends raised eyebrows. None of our friends ever criticized us for adopting Nati. That's not especially surprising; you can publicly announce you don't much like Mom, apple pie, and the American flag without anyone getting all that upset, but few people are willing to come out against giving a home to a child living in an orphanage in Africa.

But still eyebrows were raised. And this time, the questions were less easy to dismiss. "Are you worried about how Clay and Grace will handle this kind of change?" "What if this new kid is difficult?" "What kind of effect might this have on your children?" Most of the questions centered on Clay. Again, people were kind enough to point out exactly what we should be worried about. Clay hated change. What if this much change was just too much for him? It was a reasonable question, and for us, it was a terrifying one. Because, like a great many parents we knew, we believed in bubble-wrapping.

When I was a kid, every now and again, my mother would get very strict and demand that I wear a seat belt in her car. Mostly, though, she, like every other parent I knew at the time, didn't make too big a fuss about seat belts. No one I knew wore a helmet while riding a bike. When I was a teenager, there was a smoking bathroom in my high school so that kids had a place to sit and smoke a few cigarettes between classes. Honest to God, when I tell my kids stories like that now, they think that my grade-school recesses were spent having shoot-outs in the O.K. Corral.

Don't get me wrong. I'm a big fan of bike helmets, not letting kids run while holding scissors, and forcible applications of sunscreen. And if their school ever decided to create a special bathroom where the kids could have a cigarette between classes, I would join every other parent I know in dismantling the school brick by brick. I would wrap my children in bubble wrap every time they leave the house for their own protection and feel wholly justified in doing so. What gets a bit trickier is when I try to bubble-wrap my kids to protect them from their own emotional lives.

WE'D MET WHEN OUR CHILDREN were toddlers.

Clay and our friend's son were close; soon we found out that Clay's new friend had a sister our daughter's age. I got along with the dad, Mary with the mom. There were eight of us total, two sets of four that matched perfectly. Our kids played so well that sometimes all four adults could eat together and actually talk to each other.

When we decided to adopt Nati, our friends said all the usual things about how wonderful that was, what a great thing we'd be doing, how kind we were. But added with those comments were the questions about how our kids would react. Would they be okay?

When we finally chose a specific child to adopt, we showed them, and all of our friends, the videos and pictures we had of our new son, Nati. Clay told our friend's son about Nati; the next time they came over, our friends showed their son a picture of Nati, saying, "This is going to be Clay's new brother. Remember how we talked about Clay's getting a new brother and about how we're not going to do that?"

Bubble wrap. It's the language we used to use for our kids. It's how we tried to keep them safe and cocooned. "Don't panic, this is not a change we'll do." "This is your friend's new house. We're not moving." "Look at how pretty that room is now that it's been painted, but we're not going to change your room." For some, it's a way of being kind and gentle and loving. For me, it's more of an act of self-defense. Point out that you like some change in another kid's life without telling your kid that you don't plan to change the same thing in his life and you have to spend hours calming him or her down. "I just said I like Sam's haircut; you don't have to get the same one. No, I'm not saying I like Sam's head better than I like yours; I like you best always. I just said . . ."

We all got together for dinner not too long after I came back from Ethiopia with Nati, and it went well. After a while, the girls went back upstairs; Clay and his friend began to play ball again. Nati wandered off to play with whatever toys he could find.

More talk, more playing, until finally, for some reason, our friend's son went up to his room. Nati had been playing quietly but had picked up a few toys that were "special." Things that had been built with Lego had come apart; stuff had been moved. Kids are sensitive; Clay and Grace had special toys, too.

Our friend's son got upset. Fair enough. Honestly, I'm a full-grown adult and sometimes I still get cranky when people mess with my stuff. His mother comforted him, and we apologized. That was fair, too. Her son was upset and she comforted him. Parents tend to want to protect their children from the world. We want to shield our kids from upset, hurt, and turmoil. And, at that moment, my family was pretty tumultuous.

In the end, our two families didn't fight or have a huge breakup. We just found ourselves hanging out less and less. The eight of us didn't fit together quite so well now that there were nine of us. We were now a louder, more chaotic family. Our friends had asked us if we'd been worried about how Nati would affect our kids, but in a short period of time, they'd decided that their kids would be the ones who'd be better off without all the noise, clutter, and chaos we'd come to represent.

And I get it. I get it entirely, because whenever I'm given the option, I try to protect my kids. But once we adopted Nati, we lost that option. And often I mourned the loss of our bubble-wrapped kids. Unlike Nati not knowing English, which turned out to be more of a small obstacle than a huge emotional issue, or overt racism, which we tended not to encounter all that much, my inability to bubble-wrap my kids, to keep them from the scary effects of uncertainty and change, was something that was real and felt incredibly dangerous. I was playing with Clay's and Grace's futures and I had no way of knowing what would happen. We'd decided, on a whim, to adopt a child who was so different that we worried that every single part of their childhoods and futures would be compromised or even destroyed.

What happened instead was what I came to think of as the Great Sneaker Miracle—though it was a bit slower in coming together than your average miracle.

The first few months Nati was here went fine for Clay and Grace. It was exciting and dramatic and a whirlwind. Nati was a source of fascination and fun and laughter to them both. Then, after about three months, Clay started getting annoyed with Nati. There were sporadic arguments about toys being taken, and about having to share video games. Nati, who sometimes seems to think talking is part of the breathing process, had begun blurting out comments just as Clay was in the middle of telling a story or asking a question and it was driving Clay nuts. Nati, too, was instantly popular with all the kids at school, which made Clay feel threatened and insecure.

And yet I could still see that Clay loved Nati. They were forming a reasonable relationship; they weren't happy together all the time, but they genuinely seemed to get along.

And as Clay and Nati got past their private honeymoon period, Gracie and Nati began doing more things together. Clay was doing more homework and had less time after school; before long Mary and I got used to seeing Grace and Nati drawing together or working on quiet projects.

Okay, the part about the sneakers . . .

It was after Nati had been here about four months; Clay and Nati's honeymoon was over, but they still were (and are) friends. Or perhaps that's not the right word; what they are, oddly enough, are brothers. They crack each other up, annoy, and love each other in turns.

And then, Clay needed new sneakers.

At age five, my daughter had—and I think I've got this right—799,628 pairs of shoes, boots, sneakers, sandals, and slippers. She had more pairs of shoes in her closet than I've owned over the entire course of my life. Clay, on the other hand, had one pair of shoes. It was the same style of sneaker he had worn since he was five, three years before. One day, when Clay was six, Mary and I told him we'd have to get a new pair of sneakers. He'd been so determined to avoid change of any kind, even just changing his shoes, that his toes could be seen sticking out of the pair he wore every day. He was so anxious about change that when I dragged him into a shoe store, I had to pin him down while the salesman put the sneakers on his feet. Sometimes I still have nightmares. As does the salesman, I'm sure.

So when I say my son hated change, I really mean it. He. Hated. Change. A lot.

Clay had been six when I'd held him down at that shoe store, but to my eye, he hadn't changed much in the years since then which, come to think of it, shouldn't be that surprising, what with him hating change, and all.

So Nati had been with us a few months. Clay needed sneakers. I gritted my teeth and told him we'd have to go to the shoe store.

And then, the Great Sneaker Miracle occurred.

Clay looked at his feet and agreed he needed new sneakers. We went and bought him sneakers.

And that was it—a small but indisputable family miracle.

No fights. No screaming. No problem with change.

I couldn't stop myself from pointing out to Clay how much he'd changed. He shrugged and then admitted it was pretty hard to get worked up over a new pair of sneakers after you'd found a way to get used to a whole new brother.

And that was our miracle. That was when I knew that Clay and Grace were not only going to be all right, but they were going to be better than just all right; they had grown and changed because we'd adopted Nati.

We'd worried so much that bringing a new child into our family would harm our kids that it had never really occurred to either of us that it might help them. Yes, we had abstract ideas about how adopting Nati might help our kids become

more charitable, but we simply hadn't foreseen or been able to imagine the many, smaller changes that would take place. Somehow, the crystal ball I thought I had when it came to my children's futures turned out to only be able to supply me with scary possibilities that might never actually occur. I certainly wasn't capable of seeing the small good things that might be hiding around the corner. We didn't know that Clay would loosen up or that Grace would learn to express herself both more calmly and more forcibly because Nati was there. Years later, when Clay was well into his teen years, he told me that because he'd gotten a brother who was so loud and extroverted, he'd learned to become more extroverted too and that had it not been for our adopting Nati, he'd never have had a life filled with so many good friends and goofy fun. We didn't know that would happen, but how could we have?

That's the thing about worry: Most of us are really bad at it. We worry about the wrong things almost all the time. I have worried about thousands of things over the course of my children's lives, and I have been wrong about almost all of them. That's not to say that my children haven't had problems. It's just that I never saw any of those problems coming, possibly because I was too busy worrying about stuff that never happened. That map we all think we have of the minefield tends to be almost totally useless as a real-life navigational tool.

Nati, by the way, was not immune to that syndrome. When he first arrived, he took every opportunity to let us know that he, in his words at the time, "loves the Jesus." It was clear that even though he didn't know much about religion, someone had spent a lot of time convincing him that the way into our hearts would be to say those words. One day, when we were visiting New York early on, I took the kids to St. Patrick's Cathedral. Every time we saw a stained-glass window, Nati would make sure to tell me that he "loved the Jesus." I'd smile, nod, and tell him that was great, and then he'd run off, totally and completely uninterested in the window, the church, or anything else on that general subject. Next picture, no matter what of, he'd run over to me and tell me again that he "loved the Jesus." Finally, there was an announcement over the church PA that services would start soon. Nati, who was never sure what those words meant, looked up, mystery finally solved, and said to me, "Dad, is that the Jesus?" It was a long time before I got the heart to tell him that he'd been adopted into a family of Jews.

And that's the problem with worrying. Not that it's so very wrong to be worried—there are, after all, plenty of things that can go wrong in the world—but rather that I'm so bad at knowing what those things will turn out to be. I'd been anxiously preparing all sorts of problems connected to racism, language, and my two youngest kids, and none of those things had turned out to be that big of a deal. On the other hand, I'd completely ignored what turned out to be a very real and difficult problem.

Nati was just too damn happy.

And confident. Way, way too confident.

I know that it would be easy to say, "Well, of course he's happy, he just got out of an orphanage." I know that when I say Nati was too damn happy and confident, it sounds like I'm setting up for some sort of dumb joke, but truly and honestly, I'm not.

Nati was just way too damn happy.

And confident. Way, way too confident.

One day when I was picking up the kids after school, I spoke to Nati's gym teacher. He told me that Nati was causing problems in PE by trying to get the class to play different games than the one the teacher wanted them to play. It seemed that when the teacher said it was time to play soccer, Nati argued and then tried to get everyone to play tag instead.

Or tetherball.

Or, you know, whatever game he thought they should play.

Now that he's older, Nati has stopped trying to persuade his PE teachers to play different sports, but his confidence goes on unabated. A few weeks ago, we were talking about politics and how even the president of the United States had to deal with the opposition party, and the voters, media, and lobbyists when he tried to get something done. Nati thought it over and then told me he wouldn't want to be president. When I asked why not, he told me, "The president doesn't have enough power." Being a dictator, Nati felt, would be much more to his liking.

We had worried about how to defend a poor, sweet, or-phaned child from racism and the hardships of a world that didn't speak his language. What we hadn't prepared for was the fact that we had adopted a child with the confidence of a four-star army general and the charisma of a young Elvis. Singing and dancing in the morning, interrupting every con-versation with something he thought was way more interest-ing than whatever else we were talking about, and telling people exactly how to do things he'd never done in his life. In everything he did, Nati was a joyous, exuberant, dazzling pres-ence. And it made me crazy.

Nati spent his afternoons dragging Clay from room to room telling him what games to play and how. We'd been a family that had gotten used to working things out by finding a consensus. If I hadn't happened to make dinner on, say, a Sunday night and one kid wanted to go out to eat and one kid wanted to stay in and order a pizza, we'd let the kid who wanted to stay in pick the restaurant we ate at, or let the kid who wanted to go out pick the TV show to watch after we ate at home. It all worked fairly well, but suddenly things were moving in a new direction because Nati always had a preference and he wasn't shy about shouting it out.

"Clay, Grace, do zis! With paper!" he'd say when he wanted everyone to draw with him.

"No, everyone here!" when he wanted us all to go with him from one room to another.

"I want French House!" when he wanted to eat. (A note of explanation might be useful here. Nati didn't care much about architecture; he just hadn't figured out that the food he loved most was called a French fry and not a "French House." At least, that's what I assumed. I mean, he was usually pretty happy when I gave him French fries after he'd asked for a French House, but then, maybe it was just a bargaining technique. You want some French fries so you ask for a château in Provence and then just pretend you're "settling" for the fries.)

Had I thought to write a list of every fear I had about adopting a child, I would not have written one single word about how worried I was that my new son would be too confident, too bold, too goofy, and too silly. I would not have ever been able to imagine that Nati would cause confusion and conflict in our home not because he was so sad or needy or afraid, but because he was so determined, excited, and energetic.

They say that if you spend ten thousand hours practicing something, you'll master it. So my question is this: Why am I not better at worrying? I've spent way, way more than ten thousand hours being anxious about stuff that might happen one day in the future, and yet somehow I, and almost every other parent I know, almost never worry about the right things. Or, as Mark Twain once put it, "I've had many troubles in my life, some of which actually happened."

Still, I should be better at it. After all, I learned how to worry at the feet of a master.

I don't want to indulge in stereotypes. To imply that any religious or ethnic group is universally cheap, prone to gambling or drunkenness, unusually stupid, or bad at driving would be idiotic. So the fact that my mother gasps in panic each and every time anyone she's related to sneezes, coughs, or even yawns has, I'm sure, nothing to do with the fact that she's Jewish. Honestly, I really don't know for sure that she's any more anxious than any other parent; after all, I've never been raised by someone who wasn't a Jewish mother. What I do know is that my mother has been in a state of constant anxiety since 1945. My mother is a Pez dispenser that serves up fear instead of candy. When one worry ends, a new one pops right up to take its place. She worries about me, my sister, my children, my sister's children, and the possibility that my sister's children might think that the fact that I just wrote that she worries about my children before I wrote that she worries about my sister's children will make my sister's children think she doesn't worry about them as much as she worries about my kids. Which she does.

She worries that I'm not eating enough, that my wife is working too hard, that Nati isn't working hard enough, and that I might drive in the rain when everyone knows that the roads where I live get slick when they're wet. My mother worries a lot. More important, she thinks that worrying is a good thing. A responsible thing. The right thing. Worrying is how you show you care. Worrying is how you protect the people you love. Worrying is, to my mother, and to most parents I know, *useful*.

When I grew up, it was made very clear to me that you were supposed to worry. If you'd gotten a bad grade on a test, it wasn't enough to study or meet with your teacher. You were also expected to be unhappy. Life was serious business and if you sat around feeling happy and relaxed all day, you'd never get anywhere. It's what I learned from my well-intentioned parents and it's what I believed. And so, before Nati came, I worried.

I worried about language and racism and the effect of massive change on my very change-resistant son, and I was wrong about every worry I had. Because even though I learned all about worrying from two people who I'm fairly certain both majored in worry in college, it turns out what I'm not very good at is knowing what to worry about. Which sort of makes the whole worrying thing a little pointless.

I spent years, by the way, judging my mother's near-constant state of panic, until, that is, I became a parent myself. After I had children, I realized that a lot of what had seemed to be misguided ideas about how to raise a child were actually just the sorts of things you say when you love something more than feels safe, when your desire for someone else's well-being takes you well past rational thought. (Or when you're just exhausted, hungry, and doing the best you can. At some point I realized I would have to either forgive my parents for the weird stuff they'd done as parents, or start blaming myself a lot more for the weird stuff I was doing as a parent. Before I had kids of my own, I used to suspect my parents had some sort of master game plan for warping my mind, as if they'd looked into my crib and said, "What a sweet baby. Let's make him crazy." Now I realize that in all the noise and chaos of raising kids, every father at some point is bound to say some pretty crazy stuff. Turns out getting tired and frustrated enough to say to your own child, "If you don't stop making so much noise, I'm going to start screaming my head off!" is way more effective than going to therapy when it comes to getting over your own childhood angst.)

For years, one of my mother's biggest fears was about whether I'd ever get married. I wasn't especially skilled at

relationships when I was younger, so my mom very helpfully made sure to tell me that she was spending as much of
her free time as possible being anxious that I would die alone.
Then one day I met Mary, and we've been together for more
than two decades. Problem solved—though, of course, that
wasn't the only time my mother worried needlessly. When I
went to sleepaway camp for the first time, she literally ran
alongside the bus and shouted up to me that I absolutely must
not forget to eat. (I was going away for two months. Eventually I'd have remembered.) On the other hand, what she ne-
glected to warn me about before I left for that trip was that
if I had a stomachache for two days accompanied by a high
fever, I should have my appendix taken out as quickly as possible. That would have really come in handy that summer.
And if my mother doesn't know how to worry, trust me, the
rest of us have very little chance of doing it right either.

When everyone was busy asking me if I was sufficiently
worried about not being able to communicate with my new
son, no one bothered to ask me if I was worried about how I'd
handle raising a child who had so much innate confidence
that he gets frustrated I won't let him choose how I invest his
college fund. And if it's really true that the things I worry
about don't tend to happen, but the things I never know I
should worry about do sometimes happen, wouldn't that also
mean that I'm so bad at worrying that it's almost not worth
the effort? Oh, and by the way, Nati has asked me to tell you
that he's not kidding about the college fund and that when he

invested some of his own money in the stock market not too long ago, he did better at it than I did. Seriously, who could have seen that coming?

More and more I find myself dividing the things I worry about into two categories. First, there's group A, the stuff that I think will bring about total cataclysmic ruin and destruction. Disease. Texting while driving. Global warming. And, on days when I'm especially amped up, zombie apocalypse. Grace, I fear, would be especially ill suited for fighting zombies.

Then there's group B, the smaller stuff that I think will merely ruin my kids' lives. The B list is longer and includes, but is certainly not limited to, the amount of time my kids spend studying versus the amount of time they should spend studying, my belief that they'd all get into better colleges if they'd only run for class president, my concern that Clay doesn't get enough vitamin B in his diet, my strong suspicion that Nati's habit of falling asleep in his pants will leave him both perpetually exhausted and forever wrinkled, my unflagging belief that relying on using emoticons while texting will limit Grace's ability to one day communicate effectively while at college or work, and my occasional worries that I'd be a much better parent if I forced all three of my kids to use all the time they spend playing games on their phones reading great Russian novels that I have not read yet myself, but fully intend to read soon. And so on.

When it comes right down to it, I worry on the one hand about death, and on the other hand about all the stuff that might happen to them if they somehow survive being teenagers. Which covers most everything.

Oddly enough, I'm fairly certain that the dramatic over-the-top fears I have about death are the more useful of the two types of fears. Because when I worry about things that I know are far, far beyond my control—earthquakes, zombies, and the like—I tend to quickly remember that all that's really happening is I'm feeling anxious because I love my kids so much that the thought of losing them is too much for me to bear. On the other hand, when I have a fear that presents itself as rational analysis, then I feel like I should act on it. I should urge my son to do more after-school activities; I should push him and prod him and make him miserable so that one day he'll be happy. The fears that seem sane are the ones that always wind up making everybody crazy.

Clay is eighteen now. Yes, I worried about what college he'd get into. But that worry was tempered by the fact that I have absolutely no way of knowing what his successes and failures in life will be or what will cause them. I know adults who went to Ivy League colleges and then became unhappy lawyers, and I know college dropouts who managed to get paid good money to review movies on the radio (okay, that was me). Do I worry that my kids won't get into a "good enough" school and that because of that, they won't be able to get a job they love? Maybe, but then again, if all of my experiences with Nati are any guide, then I may well be worrying about the wrong thing. Honestly, for all I know, I ought to be worrying that my kids won't get into the "wrong" college since that might be where they'd meet the right mate or a future business partner. Or maybe I could just skip the worrying part altogether.

I used to think if I was anxious it meant that I had to fix the problem I was worried about. Now I think if I'm worried it's because I love my kids and that's how it comes out sometimes. Which means I can just feel my feelings of anxiety without chasing after them like a dog chasing a car. The fact that parents worry that if their kids fail their fourth-grade spelling tests it'll establish a lifelong pattern of sloth, bad study habits, and underachieving that will forever haunt their attempts to do well in work and relationships doesn't actually mean that those parents should be screaming at their kids to study spelling more. It means that parents worry and that maybe the best thing they can do for their kids is not to worry so much. The problem isn't the spelling test and it probably isn't even the kid's reaction to the spelling test . . . it's the raw panic that the spelling test makes the parent feel.

The problem, in short, isn't always what our kids are or aren't doing. Sometimes the problem is only our reaction to what our kids are and aren't doing. The problem is our fear-based reaction. Yes, kids should study for tests. And yes, as a parent, I try to make a space, both physically and emotionally, where my kids can do their work as best they can, but when I find myself nagging, arguing, and in general flipping out, then the problem is usually me.

Most of my fear is, after all, rooted in the arrogance that I know what is best. I know the right schools, friends, and activities for my kids, and if they veer off the path I've chosen for them, I get worried, because after all, I also know what the future holds. But if I look at my track record and see how often I am wrong, I can realize I am just afraid. In general, I am a frightened person. The cure for that tends to involve deep breathing, staying in the moment as best I can, and not—repeat, not—trying to control every square inch of my kids' lives.

You know what gesture people make when they want to show someone is crazy? They point their fingers at their heads and then rotate that finger in small tight circles near their ear, round and round in an endless loop. Well, there's a good reason that's how we indicate that someone is nuts. That endless loop is exactly what crazy looks like. If I wake up one day convinced that my son needs to take cello lessons to get into a good college so he can have a good job and a happy life, I then have to find him the best possible cello teacher and then I have to demand that he practice every day without fail until he's been admitted to Harvard. My son starts to lose interest in the cello, but I know what's best and so we argue each and every day, and I wind up losing all the happiness either of us might have had today in order to guarantee him a lifetime of cello-playing, Ivy-League-college-attending bliss later on. Round and round I go with no sign of an exit.

Or.

Or I can just say to myself that while yes, I do want my son to go to a good college, cramming a cello into his life may not be the only way to accomplish that. I can begin to breathe, relax, and accept the notion that my blinding insight that learning the cello is the best way to guarantee him an adult life of ease may not be correct. It may just be fear. The answer to fear isn't to try to solve problems that may not exist. It's to relax and find just a little bit of faith that my kids will find their own paths in life. Fear is like a smudge on your glasses. No matter where you look, it tends to be all you see.

I'm pretty convinced that the reason it's so hard to give up worry is that it feels productive. Sure, I can't control my kids' futures, but being anxious at least gives me the illusion of being in charge. And if fear worked, if it actually helped us make better decisions, then worry and panic would be the absolutely right emotions for any parent to revel in. That real problems have almost always blindsided me while the things that have kept me up at two A.M. never seem to happen should tell me something, but far too often I feel like being anxious is productive. Besides, what am I supposed to do, *nothing*?

Well . . . no. You still have to feed your kids and buy them clothes and worry about them and what they're doing. I know that there are parents who are guilty of true neglect, but let's go ahead and assume that no parent who leaves their four-year-old alone so they can fly to Vegas for the weekend is going to bother reading this book. Or, to make it even simpler, if you're worried you're not worrying enough, trust me, you're worrying enough.

No matter how hard you try to not try so hard, you'll still wind up cajoling, pushing, and sweating all sorts of things. But if you're worried that not believing all your fears will lead you to not worrying enough . . . well then, you're worrying more than enough. Really, I promise.

Personally, I don't try not to worry. What I do work at is not listening to everything my mind tells me. I can't stop myself from being anxious about my kids and their futures, but I can remind myself that I've never been all that good at predicting their futures. The trick is to hear what's going on in my head without listening to it as if it were the most important thing in the world. Because while I can't stop myself from overthinking, I certainly don't have to believe everything I tell myself.

Fortunately, every parent has had some practice at hearing without listening. I love Clay more than life itself, but when he was seven he once told me about a video game he'd played with his friend, and I'm almost certain the story didn't finish up till he was ten. I nodded my head and smiled and said, "Uh-huh," over and over. Now, I try and do that to myself when I start getting anxious.

"If Grace doesn't stop freaking out about math she's never going to get through her SAT in a few years," I tell myself.

"Uh-huh," I respond.

"If Clay doesn't stop checking his phone every ten minutes and actually do his summer reading, he's going to get off to an awful start to the year and the teachers will all form really negative opinions and then—"

"Uh-huh."

And so on. I hear myself, but that doesn't mean I have to listen. It's like being in an elevator that plays bad Muzak. I can't turn the noise off, but I certainly don't have to dance along. Because I've learned that there's a part of me that will always be convinced that it's easier to have a problem than it is to have a feeling. I can feel all the vulnerability that comes with loving something as much as we love our kids; I can feel the rawness that comes with all that love or I can make up problems about what may or may not happen to my kids somewhere down the road and then try to solve those problems even though they don't exist yet. But I don't anymore, because I've learned that those problems tend to really just be distractions.

Because what's left, after the worrying, the controlling, the nagging, and the fighting over things that turn out not to matter that much, is the stuff that actually matters. Loving your children. Getting to spend time with your children that both you and they will cherish. Being with them.

I'm sure that there are times when prodding my kids more would be good. On the other hand, when I'm not captive to my every fear, when I don't believe that my fears are useful and informative, I allow my children to be independent. When I stop helicoptering over them, they can finally learn to fly.

And the things I did worry about? Well, oddly enough, they're some of my happiest memories. I think about Nati's first day of school, when he'd been here all of three months. I'd given his teachers cheat sheets with a few words of Amharic, including, of course, the word *shent*. And so when Nati began to shout at me, "Dad, peet! Peet!" I worried that he'd entered some sort of gray area between two languages and that he'd be unable to communicate something as basic as his need to pee.

I corrected him and said, "No, Nati, pee-pee." He corrected me and said, "No, Dad, peet! Peet!" I wondered if there was someone named Pete in the class, but the grade was filled with kids with names like Dylan and Miles, with not a Pete in sight.

"*Shent*, Nati?" I asked him.

"No pee!" he said.

I assumed that this meant he had to pee, but simply didn't want to.

"Nati, *shent*," I told him.

"No, Dad," he said, "Nati peet, Nati peet!"

"Yes, Nati, *shent*," I told him.

"No peet," he said.

"Right," I agreed. "*Shent*, peet, same thing. Go *shent* peet."

Nati shook his head. Not that I could blame him. At that point I wasn't sure what I was saying either.

I took a deep breath and asked, "Nati, no *shent*?"

He pointed outside, where some easels were set up.

"No, Dad, Nati peet please!"

He wanted to paint. All my anxiety, fear, and worry had led Nati and me into something no more harmful than an Ethiopian version of Abbott and Costello asking each other, "Who's on first?" It's one of my favorite memories. For Nati, it's less than that, since it's just a story I tell him about a day he forgot years ago.

All that worrying turned out—surprise, surprise—to be hardly worth it. Which is why I find that, more and more, I'm unwilling to listen to everything my head tells me I need to panic about. Which leaves me more and more time to enjoy my children and my life. This is, after all, your life, the one life you're going to get. If you miss twenty years of it in a state of constant anxiety about your children's future, you'll not only have lost some of your best years, but even worse, you'll have spent twenty years teaching your child exactly how to throw away twenty years of their lives panicking about their children.

The problem, of course, is that some worries are worth worrying about. And since it's almost impossible for me to know which worries are worth listening to, once again, and which aren't, I have to rely on the power of my first words, instead of insisting on the right to have the last ones.

Yes, I can choose to believe that my fears are full of wisdom, but there's very little joy in that sort of a life. By trusting in the power of the example I set by living my life productively, responsibly, and kindly, all in front of my children, and by having faith in the ongoing conversation that is our daily life, I become free from the obligation to obey my every fear's whims.

I have to trust that my kids will respond better to the sight of my positive example than they do to the sound of my shrill nagging. I have to have faith that a child who sees their parents participating fully in a life that engages them will follow that example and do more good and constructive work in their own life than a child whose parent demands they practice an instrument that they don't want to play so that they can be happy years and years down the road. And when I can't get myself to trust that my kids will do what's best, I can always go back to reminding myself that my ability to predict the worst is rarely foolproof.

That's a difficult task. There is nothing in this world quite so seductive as our own fears. And the idea that I can fight those fears off by first recognizing the limits of my own knowledge, and second, by hoping that my day-to-day behavior around my children will be enough to influence their lives, seems like a very shaky ladder on which to climb. And yet I know that spending my life obeying my every fear is not much of a plan either. I know that when I parent out of fear, I create nothing but more fear and a less stable and happy home for the people I love. It's easy to put more faith in the power of anxiously shouting at your kids to stand up straight, do their homework, and practice their tuba than in the power of actually being and behaving like the person I want to be, showing my child how to be kind, responsible, and sensible by living clearly and visibly in front of them. The problem is, parenting out of fear just doesn't work.

Clay is eighteen and has never once stayed out past his curfew. That's because he's a responsible, decent, honest kid. Also, because he doesn't have a curfew. The thing about drawing lines in the sand is that people tend to wind up on the wrong side of them. If I say to Clay, "Be home by eleven P.M. or you'll be punished," there will be times when he'll be driving home far too quickly at 10:55 to make sure he doesn't get in trouble. There will, in all likelihood, be times when he's going to be very distracted while he drives home at eleven thirty trying to think of ways to sneak into the house so I don't know he's late.

I understand the reasoning behind curfews. Very little good has happened in this world after two in the morning. Interestingly enough, though, I can't recall my son ever being out quite that late anyway. What I can recall, however, are the times when Clay has said he's thinking of going out and I've been able to suggest that he looks tired and that maybe he'd feel better if he had an early night. I know that may sound roughly as realistic as seeing a cartoon Snow White getting small birds to do her laundry, but when you remove confrontation and seemingly arbitrary and fear-driven rules from your life, you create a space for actual conversation. If you can avoid saying, "You have to be home at eleven P.M. because I say so and what I say goes," you might have a child who will occasionally listen to you when you ask, "When's your paper due? Are you going to be too tired to get it done on Sunday?" And no, that doesn't mean that your child will automatically do what you want them to do. But if getting your child to obey you is your goal, I can only wish you the best of luck and promise you that should you succeed I will attend the parade honoring your historic achievement. Me, I just want a kid who can make his own commonsense choices. Sometimes my kids, like all people, make the wrong choices. Usually they don't. What I want is to influence their choices, not to make them myself.

It's not that I'd rather be my children's friend than their father. Like every other parent of a kid with a driver's license, I worry about him texting, drinking, and driving with friends who are irresponsible. I'm not willing to give up my authority as a parent just to maintain a false sense of harmony. What I am interested in is what works and what doesn't work.

Because I am aware that I get nowhere when I listen to my fears, I've become more willing to trust in the notion that I can best raise responsible, intelligent children by keeping open lines of dialogue and modeling sane and sensible behavior rather than nagging, yelling, and dictating rules they don't understand and will spend their lives trying to circumvent. I suppose that seems radical. If so, that's a little sad.

And yes, for the record, I am terrified that having written

all of that, my son will be arrested for robbing a bank at three A.M. when he would have been home if only I'd set a curfew. Also, I saw a small bug in my bathroom this morning and I'm pretty convinced we'll have to spray thousands of dollars' worth of pesticides all over our house and that some of them will cause me to become ill. Because knowing that my fears tend not to be accurate doesn't mean I don't have fears. It means I can choose to ignore them as best I can. And that means I can enjoy watching my children learn to become adults.

And in the end, calmly loving and cherishing your child is more than *bakka*. It's everything.

# THERE ARE NO APPLES ON OAK TREES

*How Trying to Turn My Ethiopian Son*

*into a Neurotic Jew Taught Me*

*It's Nature, Not Nurture*

MY SON HAD A BEARD THE DAY WE MET.

Or so I thought at the time. Really. My very first thought the first time I ever laid eyes on Nati was, "Huh, I didn't know he had a beard."

He didn't. Of course he didn't. Five-year-olds don't grow facial hair. I should have taken that first look at him and thought to myself, "I wonder why my son has a string attached to his chin."

But I was tired from flying halfway around the world, sick to my stomach, and more scared than I'd ever been because I was about to meet a five-year-old Ethiopian boy, spend two weeks with him, and then fly home and spend the rest of my life, every single day of it, being his father.

So I thought he had a beard.

Stitches. What he had, of course, were stitches.

Nati had run into a table and someone at the orphanage had done such a poor job of giving him stitches that they'd left the string used to sew up his cut dangling from his face.

If I'd known why Nati needed stitches that day, I'd have been able to answer one of the most basic questions every parent wonders about. But I thought he had a beard, which is too bad, because if I'd been just a little bit more focused I might have saved Nati and myself six or seven years of trouble.

. . .

HERE'S WHAT IT WAS LIKE the week I met my son.

I flew about halfway around the world and checked into a surprisingly nice hotel in Addis Ababa, Ethiopia. The hotel had a wonderful lobby and a very pleasant uniformed door- man. Outside, across the street from the hotel's beautiful front lawn, was a muddy not-quite road, lined with tin huts. There didn't seem to be any real sort of sewage system across the street from my hotel, so while the older people sat by the huts, all day, every day, the children played alongside unimaginable filth. I ate dinner at a nice restaurant in the hotel, slept well, and then woke up with just enough of a churning stomach so that I was, for almost the entire time I was in Ethiopia, unable to be more than ten feet from a bathroom.

When I got to the orphanage that had been Nati's home for the last six months, I got out of my cab and saw a boy standing alone, waiting for me. I recognized him from the pic- tures we'd been sent for the last few months, saw that he'd grown a beard since his last photo, and then Nati walked up to me. As I knelt to him, he wrapped his arms around me and put his head on my shoulder and allowed his full body to sag into mine. We'd known each other for less than sixty seconds and he had already decided he was home.

In that moment I became his father and he became my son. A great deal of laughing, yelling, frustration, happiness, misery, and joy has come and gone in the years since that day, but I know without question that it was in that moment that I first became the father of my third child.

And then I thought to myself, "Oh, that's not a beard. It's string. Why does he have string attached to his face?"

Eventually I got the story, first from the people at the orphanage, and then, months later, from Nati himself. The day before I'd come, Nati had been having a good time with his friends. He'd been laughing and running and getting very silly, when he ran, chin first, into a table. He'd been having so much fun he didn't even see that the table was there.

He had stitches. Because, again, he was too busy *laughing and playing and having fun* to see where he was going. In an orphanage. In Ethiopia. I've been to that orphanage. It was clean and the adults in charge did everything they could to love and help the kids who were living there. But there were about ten hard metal bunk beds in one tiny room where some of the kids, including Nati, slept. The classroom where they spent some of every day was small and cramped and could have induced claustrophobia in a corpse. The kids there had suffered horrible, traumatic losses that they'd be spending the rest of their lives trying to process and recover from. Yes, there was a small place to play, but it was still an orphanage and I didn't see any other kids who were having so much fun that they were running into stuff.

And just as I should have seen that string dangling from Nati's face and known that of course it wasn't a beard, I should have known right then and there the answer to that old question: Is it nature or nurture? Are our kids born the way they are, or do we make them who we want them to be? Just how much can we, as parents, mold our children?

Here's a hint. When your child is the sort of kid who can have a blast in an orphanage, you're going to have a lot less influence, power, and control than you might have hoped for.

A great deal of what we consider to be parenting is about power and control and molding our kids into what we've decided is the best version of themselves. We remind them to say *please* and *thank you*, in the hopes that they will grow into polite adults. We demand that they keep playing on the team of the sport they no longer enjoy so they can learn about hard work and persistence because we know they'll need those qualities later on in life. We demand they do chores so they'll become responsible and one day be able to (please, God) hold down a job. We spend much of their childhoods and our adult years with our hands on their shoulders, steering them this way and that, all because we are their parents and molding their characters and shaping their destinies is the whole point.

Unless it isn't.

What if all that molding and steering aren't necessary or even useful? What if our kids come into the world already formed? What's the job of a parent then? Most every parent who has at least two kids has at some point noticed that his kids are different. One kid is quieter, the other more adventurous. Some kids are natural readers; others never met a tree they didn't want to climb or cut down with the ax they plan on borrowing when no one's looking. And yet if we don't go further than just noticing that our kids seem to be born with personalities already inside them, we miss an enormous opportunity. If our kids are who they are from the day they're born, isn't it possible that our jobs as parents should be a lot more about appreciating them than molding them?

You might think that it would be difficult to get to know a child when the two of you don't speak the same language, but really, it isn't. My first week alone with Nati was spent in Ethiopia, waiting for the government there to finish processing our adoption paperwork. Nati very quickly got into the habit of running ahead of me in the halls of our hotel, hiding behind a corner, and then jumping out to try and scare me. (That tended not to work, mostly because I always saw him running ahead of me to hide but also because he always yelled "Yes!" at me instead of "Boo!" So really, he tended to look more like a very eager waiter than a scary goblin. "YES! May I help you?!") He was a ball of nonstop energy and enthusiasm from the moment he got up until the moment he went to sleep, always singing to himself and laughing about pretty much everything he came into contact with. He was a young five, and certainly unfamiliar with a lot of what the world had to offer. TV fascinated him as it does most kids, but so did the hotel escalator. None of it scared him; he seemed to treat the whole world like an amazingly cool playground built just for his amusement.

One day at the hotel, Nati ran ahead of me as we walked

into the lobby. By the time I caught up, Nati was speaking with the woman behind the counter. Then he began dancing. A moment later, the woman burst out into laughter. When I asked her to translate what he'd said that had made her laugh, she replied that my son had just told her, "Speaking English is easy for me! And I can dance, too!" When you have to tell someone that speaking English is easy in the language of Amharic, because you don't actually know how to speak English yet—well, at that point, you're really taking the concept of confidence and self-assurance into a whole new arena. If you're thinking that Nati was just anxious and filled with false bravado . . . I did, too. But it didn't take long for me to realize that there was nothing false about Nati's bravado. It was, and is, 100 percent real.

For example, Nati had been living with us in California for only two or three months when we decided to go to San Diego for a day. I strapped him into his car seat next to his brother and sister and then began to drive.

Now, before Nati came along, getting into the car and driving was a fairly simple process. First, Mary or I would decide where we wanted to go. Then, we'd tell Clay and Grace where we'd decided to go by saying something like, "This is going to be fun, we're all going to the aquarium!" Then we'd buckle everyone in and drive off. Our family dynamic was fairly simple. It may have been a bit inverted, since I was a stay-at-home dad while Mary went off to the office every day, but still, we all functioned fairly smoothly together in a reasonably traditional way. At five, Grace was in a princess stage. She was happy to go on errands with me anywhere so long as she got to wear a fabulous gown. And Clay was a rule obeyer, like Mary and me. If the teacher said hold hands when you cross the street, we held hands every time we crossed the street. Clay has always tried to do things "the right way." He doesn't eat his popcorn before the movie starts, he wouldn't dream of leaving a baseball game before it was over, and he assumed that when his mom or dad said we needed to go somewhere, we needed to go there and that was that. Simple.

And then came Nati. And simple car trips stopped being quite so simple.

On this particular day, as I turned right onto a street and began heading toward San Diego, Nati started shouting, "No, Dad, go straight!" (And yes, speaking English was turning out to be fairly easy for him, just as he'd predicted in that hotel lobby.) Nati continued to try to navigate for me, shouting out, "Go left!" and "No, turn here, Dad!" until finally I turned back to him and asked with genuine curiosity, "Have you ever been to San Diego, Nati?" Honestly, it wasn't until he asked me, "I don't know ziss. What is a sandee-aago?" that I went back to trusting my own sense of direction.

We got a lot of that sort of thing from the very beginning. The first time I threw Nati a football, a type of ball he'd never laid eyes on, he helpfully corrected my throwing motion. "No,

Dad, like ziss!" he told me. And then he threw the ball one foot in front of him directly into the ground. That didn't bother him, though. He just kept practicing his way, until he'd learned to throw fairly well.

In the end, it was a friend of ours who summed up Nati's personality best. Mary and I had taken Nati to a classmate's birthday party, where our friend Adam told us to go enjoy a cup of coffee while he made sure Nati didn't get himself hurt. When we got back to the party, we found out that Nati had found the cake, removed the frosting spelling *Happy Birthday Matthew* in lovely script, and had applied it to his own face so that he could have a frosting mustache and beard. Amazingly (and because my son is indecently charming and adorable) the stunt had gone over fairly well, not just with classmates and the birthday boy, but with our very patient friends. "Nati," Adam told us with a smile, "does things that other kids only dream of." Truer words were never spoken.

At home, we struggled. Nati is nearly three years younger than our son Clay, but he quickly got into the habit of bossing his older brother around. Mary and I began to fume. Picking up the kids after school became more and more frustrating. I'd ask about everyone's day, but I'd wind up hearing only from Nati. Nati was so exuberant, loud, and commanding that he often seemed to simply overpower everyone else through sheer force of personality.

And so Mary and I began parenting.

Or, to put it slightly less charitably, Mary and I began a

long battle to try to turn our exuberant, silly Ethiopian son into a quiet, neurotic Jew, just like us.

That's not exactly how we thought of it at the time. No, we just wanted Nati to be a tiny bit different. Quieter. Humbler. A bit less goofy. A lot more focused. Maybe . . . maybe, just a little bit less happy all the damn time. We thought it was our job to add to the traits he had that we approved of while gently removing the traits we didn't like quite as much. At the time, oddly enough, that seemed perfectly reasonable to us both.

The trouble always started early. At breakfast, after Mary had gone off to work, Clay, Grace, and I had a routine we followed every day. Kind of, sort of obsessively.

I like to eat cereal in the morning. And when I say, "I like to eat cereal," I actually mean, I have to eat cereal every morning or the whole day feels weird to me. I like to quietly read the newspaper while I eat my cereal, and yes, again, what I mean when I say, "I like to quietly read while I eat," is it makes me completely and totally crazy when people try to talk to me while I eat cereal.

Clay, like me, reads the paper. He's not as obsessive about needing absolute quiet while he eats breakfast, but I've always hoped with a little luck and practice he'll get there.

Mary likes tea. She rushes out to work on weekdays but on Saturdays and Sundays she drinks tea, out of her big cup, which we are *not* allowed to wash until the end of the day because she uses it all morning for refills. Yes, we do have other large cups, but once she's made her first cup, she likes to keep that cup and no, I don't know why. But that's the rule and I accept it.

Grace is a little bit less obsessive about her breakfast routine. She eats, sometimes reads, but, like Mary, Clay, and me, she is fairly quiet about it all. When she was little I almost never heard her walking up to the breakfast table. I'd just glance over and there she'd be, quietly deciding what she wanted that day.

I tend not to think of myself as, you know, crazy, when it comes to my mornings, but there's no sense in denying that I have a pretty rock-solid routine and I get more than a little out of sorts when it gets changed. Which I suppose is how most neurotic people feel about the stuff they're neurotic about. As a whole, we were a quiet family that liked to start our mornings off as gently and smoothly as we possibly could.

Nati, on the other hand, has never been a big fan of things going smoothly.

Which is why Nati would often start the day by coming downstairs blowing air-kisses to an imaginary crowd while shouting, really shouting loudly, "THANK YOU VERY MUCH! NATI KNOBLER IZ IN ZA HOUSE!" Which is crazy as hell, but not, if you think about it, all that neurotic. Odd yes, annoyingly loud certainly, but it's not like he had one certain way he had to eat every day. That was the rest of us. Nati just wanted to have fun. Loudly. Always.

And so I tried to encourage him to maybe come down-

stairs quietly. To take a moment to think about how the other people in the house might like to, you know, ease into their mornings. And I encouraged him to read the paper, to look at the comics or at least maybe look at the photographs in the sports section. Because, I told myself, it would be good for him to grow up to be well informed.

And we worked on the shouting. There was a lot of shouting.

It was Nati's normal practice TO SHOUT AT THE TOP OF WHAT SHOULD HAVE BEEN HIS TINY LITTLE LUNGS. Every word. Or, if you prefer, EVERY WORD. Thinking I might be able to handle this particular problem with a demonstration, I stood up from the table and walked a foot or so away. The kids and Mary all looked up at me. I turned toward Nati.

"Raise your hand if you can hear me," I said in a very quiet voice.

Everybody raised their hand.

I took a step back.

"Okay, put your hand down if you can hear me," I said in the same quiet voice.

The kids, especially Nati, giggled and then lowered their hands.

"Now," I whispered as I took about six steps backward away from the table, "raise your hand if you can hear me."

Hands went up.

I began walking back toward the table, still speaking softly.

"Nati," I said, in my quiet voice, "you really don't need to use a loud voice, okay? Because we can hear you even when you whisper."

Nati smiled and lowered his head a bit, which meant he understood and I had actually gotten through to him. I was standing next to him, so now I raised my voice TO THE SAME OBSCENELY LOUD LEVEL IT HAD BEEN WHEN HE WAS SHOUTING AT ME.

"SEE, NATI? YOU DON'T NEED TO TALK THIS LOUDLY."

Nati laughed and covered his ears.

"Daaaaaaaad," he said. He was whining, but he was doing

it quietly. Better still, he managed to stay reasonably quiet that whole meal. The next day at breakfast, however, Nati began shouting again. I sighed and stood up.

"Nati," I asked in a very quiet voice, "can you put your hand up high in the air?"

No dice this time, the kid was already on to me. He just lowered his head and smiled, then raised his head back up. "NO, DAD, NO PUT MY HAND IN THE AIR," he said. "I CAN'T HEAR YOU."

And so I began shouting at Nati. But only to get him to quiet down.

There is, I think, no moment quite as goofy for a parent as when they catch themselves screaming at their child that they "WANT SOME PEACE AND QUIET RIGHT NOW, DAMMIT!" It's not an uncommon moment, but for some reason the utter insanity of screaming for quiet never seems to teach us that this business of trying to change our kids is doomed from the start. Maybe that's just because it's so noisy in our homes that we can't think these things through. I tend not to think that's it, though. I think that somehow or other we've all decided that being a parent means behaving in crazy ways in order to turn our children into the utterly sane creatures we've decided they should be. And so we scream for quiet and yell at them when they're unkind to their siblings (because nothing teaches kindness like being shouted at) and behave like lunatics all in order to turn our kids into sane, decent people.

Of course, Nati came to us already having gotten through

some remarkably awful events. So you could say, odd though it would sound to me, that losing his father, being given up for adoption by his ailing mother, and spending time in an orphanage had somehow conspired to turn him into an incredibly loud, cheerful, bossy kid. Besides, when I met Nati's birth mother and his aunt and the people at the orphanage, they all seemed pretty unanimous in saying that Nati has *always* been exactly who he is now.

And yet, determined to parent, I continued to try to alter his behavior. And yes, obviously, there is a place for that. Telling your child to use their "inside voice" when they're shouting in a restaurant is just common sense. (Though so is not taking kids who struggle to sit still to classy restaurants, come to think of it.) There's not much wrong with making your kids share their toys or having them try piano lessons either. But what I was after was more than just altering Nati's behavior: I was trying to change who Nati was. And having good intentions doesn't make the impossible any more possible.

Part of the problem was my expectations. Not surprising perhaps since, as we all know, expectations are nothing more than what resentment looks like when it's a fetus. When we decided to adopt a child, we figured we'd be doing a lot of comforting. We'd assumed we'd be spending time helping our new son build up his confidence and slowly showing him the way to come out of his shell. We could never have planned that he would love practical jokes like telling his five-year-old sister that her brother Clay was waiting for her in the bathroom (he wasn't) and then, the next day, telling her that a monster was waiting for her in the bathroom (there wasn't).

We'd taken our ideas of what *we* would have been like in Nati's horrible situation and assumed that was how anyone would react. It's not so much that we had greater expectations about who Nati would be than we had about our other kids, it's just that our expectations were especially vivid. One night, when Nati had been with us not much less than a year, I saw a beautifully made, touching foreign film on television. In one scene, a young orphaned girl told her new mother that she'd been lonely before, but now she was glad because she had a mommy and daddy again. The camera lingered on the girl's hand as she moved to hold on to her new mom's sweater; her voice was tender and soft—and lying in bed with all three kids and Mary, I found myself crying.

Which would have been fine, except the film we were watching on TV that night was *Pokémon 3*. The cartoon. Based on those little cards with pictures of monsters. The sequel to the sequel. That *Pokémon 3*.

The film was about . . . actually, I don't really know what it was about, assuming that it actually was about something, and I'm almost positive that I'm the only person on earth who found it quite so moving. Certainly, I was the only one in the room having that reaction. The kids weren't exactly holding back their tears, and my wife, whom I've seen cry at commercials, magazine articles, kindergarten plays, parent-teacher conferences, and the sight of our cat playing nicely with our dog, was completely dry-eyed, if only because two minutes into *Pokémon 3* she'd wisely gone to sleep.

So why then did *Pokémon 3* leave me in tears? I mean, sure, the first Pokémon film was a classic and even *Pokémon 2* had demonstrated a stunning grasp of the human condition, but *Pokémon 3* . . . well, let's just say some of the cartoon actors were really phoning it in. But that scene, of a child tenderly holding on to her parent's sweater, thanking her for all she's done . . . isn't that the picture any adopting parent has at least somewhere in their mind? The child, in a sweet voice, touching our hand gently and saying, "I'm so happy now that I have a new daddy. . . ." And don't we all have equally unrealistic pictures in our heads featuring all our children, adopted and not? I close my eyes and I can easily summon images that I know I've had in my head for as long as I've had kids, from the beautiful thanks they'll give me on their wedding days to moving passages about me in their presidential inauguration addresses.

It's an insane image; five-year-olds are just too busy to be grateful, but there's no point in denying that some part of my brain was thinking that way. Which was a problem, because Nati was only soft and quiet and tender for a moment or two before he passed out at the end of every night (and that was only because he was exhausted from the preceding sixteen hours of running, screaming, laughing, and knocking things over).

Of course, you don't have to have adopted your kids in

order for your expectations to grow into resentments. When my daughter was four, for instance, she and a friend took ballet lessons. Her friend's mother confidently told me that she planned on having her daughter continue to take ballet until she was at least seventeen, since she felt ballet allowed girls to achieve a certain elegance, self-confidence, and poise that they couldn't acquire elsewhere. Grace lost touch with that friend but one day, years later, I happened to run into that girl and her mom. The girl, like Grace, is now a teenager. I asked if she was still doing ballet, which made Grace's old friend literally snort with laughter while her mother winced as if in pain. Grace's friend had learned that you could also learn poise and self-confidence by being the captain of your school's softball team. And her mother informed me that she had learned that assuming she'd have a daughter who'd be a natural ballerina past age five was just asking for trouble down the road.

And yet we searched in vain for a volume button on Nati, for some way to at least occasionally render him quiet and mellow and, you know, more like . . . us. For years (yes, years) I yelled at Nati to demand that he be quiet, unaware that he was changing me a lot more than I was changing him. He wasn't getting any quieter, but I was certainly louder and more short-tempered and irritable than I'd ever been before. Still, even though I was angry more than I wanted to be, I thought I was just doing my job. Surely, I thought, with just the right amount of love, attention, and yelling he'd start growing up to be the person I knew he should be.

Now, years later, I can see that when I try to change any-one, whether it's Nati, Clay, Grace, my wife, or the person driving the car in front of me, I'm doomed to fail. And then, after I've failed I have only two options. I can keep on going down the same hopeless, miserable path trying to get oranges from an apple tree, or I can give up, relax, and just enjoy the apples. Sadly, in my case, I tend to go for that first option, but that's okay, because eventually the road forks again and I'm given the same choice. I can accept the people around me for exactly who they are, or I can keep trying to change them. Give me long enough and eventually I decide, what the hell, I might as well take the people around me for who they are, as they are, right then and there. As a wise man once said, let go, or be dragged.

I made that decision about Nati when I was talking to a friend who'd also adopted a child. Frustrated and upset, more with myself than with Nati, I said, "It just feels like no matter what I do, I can't get him to change at all." My friend looked at me for less than half of a second, rolled his eyes, and said, "Yup, that's right. Now what?" And I got it.

So what happens after you decide to accept your kids? What do you do after you decide to give up what you thought was parenting?

Accepting that it really is "nature, not nurture" meant for me that I could relax and enjoy the show. When my friend had told me about Nati making his cake beard at that long-ago birthday party, he'd laughed . . . and I'd winced. He'd seen a goofy, happy kid misbehaving a bit but with absolutely no malice at all. I'd seen years ahead of wild out-of-control behavior followed no doubt by long prison sentences handed out by judges who would wave their gavels at Nati and ask, "Didn't your father ever teach you how to behave?" But when I decided it wasn't my job to change Nati, I suddenly found myself appreciating him so much more. I caught myself laughing almost all of the time. I was able to see that nothing Nati had ever done had the slightest bit of ill will. He's loud, independent, silly, and a thousand other things, but he's not mean, cruel, or hateful. What he is, is different. And different, while scary and challenging, can be, well, different.

And no, it's not just Nati. Realizing that it really was "nature, not nurture" helped me see a great deal of very misguided nurturing that I'd done as a father before Nati joined our family. I also realized just how much my own parents had wanted to change me, just a bit, just enough so that I'd be able to get the "right" kind of job and live the sort of life they wanted for me. My father had nurtured the hell out of me when I was growing up, trying to get me to be a bit more serious. My mother hadn't seen that for me, joking was a way of communicating, and she also tried heroically to get me to be less silly. Both of my parents, with nothing but love (and perhaps a bit of fear and panic) in their hearts, had tried to get me to be all sorts of things that I simply wasn't. And then I grew up and spent twelve years writing and performing silly comedy for radio stations around the world.

And if it sounds like I'm piling blame on my parents, I know that I was no different for a long time when it came to Clay and Grace. I tried to make Clay more assertive. I nagged Grace to be less serious and stressed out (nothing inspires mirth and calm more than nagging, right?). I tried to take some of Grace's focus and transfer it to Clay, giving her some of his qualities in return like a mad scientist in one of those 1950s sci-fi films where they use lightning bolts and metal tubes to switch two brains. It was only when Nati came along and I was forced to recognize the impossibility of turning a boisterous, exuberant African kid into a quiet, sensitive, neurotic Jewish guy that I also had to accept that a lot of what I was trying to do with Clay and Grace was equally insane. When I finally stopped trying to change any of my kids, I started being able to enjoy all of who they already were.

We talk to our kids about their choices and behavior, we encourage them to try new things and to keep working on them even when it gets difficult, and that's as it should be. Nurturing is a way of expressing love, right up until it becomes a demand that the people around us change in the way that we think they should. After that, it's just banging your head against a wall.

What I've come to believe is that it was never my job to change Nati, but it continues to be my job to help him be the best possible version of who he already is. He's independent, so my job is to help foster that, by allowing him to experience the joys and sometimes difficult consequences of that independence.

Sometimes that's a surprising treat. Clay is not far from college now and Nati and Grace are teenagers as well, which means I can go out for a while and leave them more or less on their own. On nights when that happens, I've usually already made dinner, but Nati doesn't always want what I've made (and no, I don't mean metaphorically. I mean, he's a meat eater and the poor kid has already seen enough California tofu and soy products to make him weep). And so, not long ago, as I left the house to run a few errands and get Grace from a friend's house, I told Nati he could order himself a pizza if he didn't want what I'd cooked. He asked if he could order from anywhere and since there are about five pizza places near us, I said yes, so long as he didn't spend more than ten dollars, he could call wherever he liked.

When I got home an hour or so later, Nati was eating what had to have been a four-pound lobster.

I think my first response was an actual squeak, like the noise one of those chew toys for dogs makes. Then, after a deep breath, I reminded Nati about how he'd agreed to order a ten-dollar pizza. Which, of course, was where I'd gone wrong. Because while I tend to color inside the lines, Nati's more of a Jackson Pollock splatter painter when it comes to rules. And so he carefully explained to me that:

(a) I'd said he could order a pizza. He'd asked if he could order from anywhere. I'd just assumed he meant any pizza place.

(b) He had only agreed not to spend more than ten dollars.

(c) He had, through a complicated series of online transactions, found a web-only, first-time-customer-special ten-dollar lobster dinner offer, which for all I know may have involved a free subscription to a magazine, an online survey, and my agreeing to file tax returns in Argentina.

What can I say? The kid's got game. Once upon a time I might have tried to "teach" him about the importance of not wasting money and of listening to the spirit as well as the letter of an adult's instructions . . . but honestly, who would I have been kidding? The kid found a great ten-dollar lobster. Whatever mistakes he'll make in life, he's still a guy who's managed to smile through things that would have broken me in half. I needed to change that why?

When Clay was not yet four, I worried about his social skills, not realizing, since he was our first, that very few four-year-olds are capable of smart, confident, cocktail party–worthy banter. He was shy and awkward and so I decided to help. To parent. At one point, desperate to make sure that he was able to comfortably fit in with the "cool" kids, I ran out and purchased an elaborate video game system. Cool kids, I felt, tended to play video games and I was genuinely concerned that if he didn't play video games he might not be able to have enough playdates and the like to make good friends and really belong.

He was four. Four years and two months before that, he'd literally been a fetus inside a womb. Four.

Looking back, I can't help but wonder what I thought "cool" four-year-olds were. Did I really believe that Clay's long-term prospects in life would be helped if he could only be invited to sit with the kids who had Buzz Lightyear sneakers that lit up when they walked? Yup, I did. I worried my son was too quiet and too shy to do well in life, and so, through a combination of buying stuff and urging him to behave in a more self-assured way, I thought I could change his life, career path, and prospects . . . *when he was four!*

Clay is now a popular, wonderful, charming teenager. He is confident and assertive in the most pleasant ways imaginable. And if anyone on this earth, including myself, were to believe that had anything at all to do with my buying him video games in preschool, they are as crazy as I was when I did that, and that's saying something. And yes, I did all of the same stuff when Grace came along, only with prettier shoes.

I worried that who my kids were wasn't going to be enough to guarantee them the very best schools, careers, and lives. I worried that Clay wasn't tough enough to succeed (again, there aren't that many competent, career-savvy four-year-olds in the world). And so I tried to parent my kids, all three of them at different times, into being new people. And for what? Just what is it that we think our kids are going to grow up into? There is, at any given moment, one president of the United States. Far, far less than half of one percent of people in this country are professional athletes. Fewer than that are working as movie stars or astronauts. Most children, sorry to say, simply wind up becoming people. They have jobs that they may enjoy and sometimes marriages that hopefully will work, but most of all they're people. Just like me and every other adult I know, they will have weaknesses and strengths and they will have good days and bad. And nothing I do as a parent will change that.

What I can do with my children is love them, enjoy them, and help them, as best I can, feel ready to be in pleasant relationships with people they love while, hopefully, working at things they like to do. I don't need to push, prod, poke, urge, or demand that they be more serious, lighthearted, outgoing, reflective, or anything else.

Acceptance takes practice. Or, in my case, failure. Years of trying to change someone and years of failing to do so. Honestly, I was lucky. Nati has always been so very much who he is, and he has always been so impervious to my efforts to change him that all I really have to do to live happily is remember that he's mine to love, not alter. I can clear his path ever so slightly, help him pursue the things that interest him, and encourage him to keep going when he's discouraged, but his path is his own. It's not for me to build.

When Nati struggled in a class a while back, he resisted getting a tutor. I'm a big fan of finding help—honestly, I'll take it wherever and whenever I can find it—but Nati, fiercely independent, insisted he would work it out. And so he failed his next test, and the one after. And having learned that I can't force him to study the way I think he should study and solve his problems the way I think he should solve his problems, I settled instead for sitting him down and telling him some of what might happen. He could fail. He could have to repeat the class. There are consequences in life. You want to work things out on your own? Fine, but failure is an option.

Nati said he'd work it out himself. I decided to let him. And so, while I quietly made plans for what I would do should he be forced out of school at age eleven, Nati went online, found video tutorials for himself, and gradually figured it out and got back up on his feet. I told him I would do anything I could possibly do to help him, including getting out of his way.

There are different answers for different kids. When Clay struggled in math, he was glad to get extra help from a tutor, to help lighten the load. Getting Clay a tutor was loving and good parenting. Demanding that Nati have one wouldn't have been. One size fits one.

There's a really awful old joke that you've heard, assuming that you're over age nine (and if you're not, what exactly are you doing reading this book?). A man goes to the doctor and says, "Doctor, it hurts when I move my arm like this. What should I do?" The doctor looks at him for a moment and then says, "Don't move your arm like that." There's a simple and undeniable logic to that joke, and yet when it comes to parenting we lose all sight of simple truths. We spend years trying to change our kids and we spend years complaining about how they don't listen to us. "Doctor, it hurts when I move my arm like this. What should I do?"

Maybe it would be easier if we tried to just balance out our own fears instead of eliminate them. We worry that if we don't try to mold our children, if we don't try to nurture them into having every trait we deem desirable, they'll grow up to be . . . not quite good enough. Not quite good enough for the best job. Not quite good enough at relationships. Not quite good enough at whatever they try to do. We must make them stronger, more assertive, less loud, funnier, more serious, calmer, more determined, or whatever else we think they must be in order to "make it." Okay, maybe that fear isn't going away anytime soon. But there's something else we should be afraid of, that we often forget to worry about entirely.

Time.

My wife and I planned our wedding for months. I don't think either of us was particularly the sort of person who'd always dreamed of a big wedding, but weddings do have a certain momentum all their own, and, well, one thing kept leading to another. We looked at a bunch of different places to hold the party before we found a nice little restaurant. My wife looked at a few dresses. We had to figure out seating and flowers and all that other stuff you have to figure out before you get to say "I do."

I loved our wedding. I had a great time and when it was over I got to be married to Mary, whom I love. So that was awesome. I got to share that day with friends and family. The band was great. I didn't eat anything, but there was food that looked pretty good. I loved it all. But one of my clearest memories of my wedding was when it ended. The party had been going for a few hours, everyone had been having fun, and then a few people came and said their good nights. And then a few more.

I was astonished.

I truly and honestly was amazed that people were leaving . . . and after only four hours! I'd spent months and months working on that day. And now, people were going to just leave? How could that be possible?

Well, I have three teenagers now and I've begun to learn something I'd never really considered. You will always be a parent, and your kids' happiness and safety will always be the most important thing in your world, but . . .

They leave. It's almost impossible to imagine when your kids are young, just as I couldn't imagine that my wedding party was going to be, at heart, just a nice three- or four-hour night, but, yeah, they leave. You want to know the truth?

Your kids are a chapter in your life; they're not the whole book.

You get them for a very short time. I won't pretend that it will always feel like a very short time. The years may fly by, but man oh man, do some of the days ever drag on. I spent one particular Sunday afternoon at the zoo with Clay that I'm convinced lasted three and a half years.

But they go. I love my parents, really I do, but we live in different cities. We see each other when we can and we talk a lot on the phone, but "a lot" really only means a few times a week. My sister, who was always a far better child than I was, lives pretty close to my folks. She sees them more often, but even that's not every day. Or every week. Because that's what happens when your kids go on to the successful, happy lives you're so desperate for them to have. They leave and call when they can.

Time. You only have so much of it with them. Which means, maybe instead of just being afraid that you're not doing enough for them, and maybe instead of just being afraid they don't have all the traits they need to become everything you want them to be, maybe, just maybe, we should remember to also be afraid of wasting the time we do have with our kids in meaningless fights, in battles that can't be won, and in trying to make apple trees into rosebushes.

Nati, Clay, and Grace were and are who they are. I can accept that and enjoy them, or I can fight that and lose the most important thing I have: the experience of loving them just as they are.

There was a nearly yearlong period after we'd decided to

adopt Nati but before the Ethiopian government gave me permission to go and bring him home. During that time, we got pictures of Nati in the orphanage. In one of the photos you can see a group of kids sitting quietly in the background, while in the front of the photo, Nati, his arms around the shoulders of two of his little buddies, has his head thrown back as he laughs hysterically. When we first got the picture, none of us knew what was happening when the photo was taken. If the photo had a caption, it would have been, "Man! I love this orphanage!" One day, after he'd been home with us for a while, Mary showed Nati the picture and asked him what was happening that day. Nati looked at the photo and told her that one of the children at the orphanage had just been adopted and that the picture had been taken at that boy's going-away party. Then Nati looked up at Mary and said in a very serious voice, "I love a party, Mom. Sooooooo much."

So far as I know, the only party that had ever been thrown for Nati before he came to America was his own going-away party at the orphanage the day he left Ethiopia with me. It was raining that day. A few rows of chairs had been set up for the kids, but no one wound up using them. There was some cake; the kids formed a line and each got a slice. The rain picked up to a sort of steady drizzle; before long all the kids had wandered inside. The only place for the kids to play outside was this dirt courtyard the size of a small driveway. I remember watching the drops of rain muddying up the area, one by one. Nati was going to be getting on a plane to live in a whole new country with a family he hadn't yet met; the other kids were either waiting for their new parents to come and get them, or just hoping that someone would choose them and get them out of there. I took pictures of all the kids who hadn't been adopted yet so they could be posted on a Web site where people who were thinking of adopting a child might take a look. The picture we'd seen of Nati laughing had been taken at a "party" like that, a sad gathering in the dirt to see a friend leave forever. I have never been at any gathering, before or since, that left me feeling so heartbroken and sad.

When Nati told Mary that he loved parties, that was the kind of party he had been thinking of. He had, somehow, through the sheer force of his will and personality, found joy in despair and a wonderful party in a squalid, dirty courtyard. He had been a loud, silly, exuberant kid in Ethiopia and he had stayed a loud, silly, exuberant kid when he'd flown across the ocean and into my life. Like all three of my kids, Nati has grown and matured, but he has also, in so many ways, stayed the same. And for that, I am now grateful. It was never my job to change who he is. Good thing too, since I was never going to be able to change him anyway.

Because that's his perfect, unalterable nature.

And it's as plain as the string on his face.

# EAT
# THROUGH
# THEIR
# EYES

*How a Piñata and Some Mushy Food*

*Taught Me Perspective*

LEARNED THE SECRET TO HAPPILY RAISING TEENAGERS AT an Ethiopian restaurant after Nati nearly starved to death when he refused to eat anything but bananas and French fries for a few months. Also, it helped when I got to watch Nati see some boys attack a statue of me with bats. It's going to take a while to explain all of that, what with the part about my friend's baby throwing up all the time, so before I get into the details, let me give you the secret. It works on everyone, not just teenagers, by the way, though it is especially good with them.

Oh, and one other thing. I look like Harry Potter. Well, I did, ten years ago, especially when I wore my glasses. Not so much that people would stop me on the street and ask me to cast a spell or anything, but there was definitely a pretty strong resemblance. I'm not super proud of that fact, but you're going to need to know it down the road a bit.

Okay, here's the secret to happily raising teenagers. It's kind of simple, really. There are three parts, though none of them made much sense to me until the Ethiopian restaurant, the all-banana-and-French-fry diet, and the kids with bats. Still, here goes.

1. Perspective is how we see the world.
2. How we see the world dictates how we behave. If,

for example, an old friend I haven't seen in years comes running at me full speed, I might laugh and get ready to hug them. If, on the other hand, I don't recognize the old friend but instead just see a stranger running toward me, I might prepare to fight, run away, or hand over my wallet. I do what I do because of how I see what I see.

3. If I can try to see how other people, including my children, see what they see, I tend not to have as many arguments.

Now, let me explain.

In the middle of the city where we live, there's a three-block stretch called Little Ethiopia, which holds some Ethiopian restaurants, a few little Ethiopian-themed shops, and a 7-Eleven. We have friends named Kevin and Lauren who, after having their son Mark also adopted a child named Haset (now called Cindy), who'd been at the same orphanage as Nati. When we made plans to see them, Little Ethiopia seemed like the perfect place to go, even though most of the people who were going to be there that night didn't really much like Ethiopian food.

When we walked into the restaurant, our friends were already seated. Oddly enough, I had met Kevin and Lauren's daughter Haset before they had. They had decided to adopt her, the same way we'd decided to adopt Nati, based on some pictures and a few seconds of video. When I left to pick up Nati my friends asked me to check in on Haset and give them some sort of report. There was no chance they were going to change their minds about the adoption; Haset was their daughter no matter what. But they did want to know if there were any medical conditions they should be preparing for.

Both Nati and Haset had been staying in the same orphanage. There were about fifteen kids there when I'd gone to get Nati. Some were infants, like Haset; five-year-old Nati was the oldest. When I'd gone, first to meet Nati and then for his good-bye party, I'd checked in on Haset. Both Lauren and Kevin had been concerned that she hadn't seemed responsive or alert on a video they'd been sent. I was busy meeting my own new son for the first time, but together Nati and I gave her about ten seconds of "kitchy-cooing"; she smiled at me right away and I quickly e-mailed Kevin and Lauren that their new daughter was happy, alert, and healthy.

Which was more than could be said about the group of us sitting at the table that night.

Grace had been complaining about having to eat Ethiopian food, which was far too spicy for her (she has, by the way, grown to love it). Nati was loud and excited, Clay was annoyed at how loud and excited Nati was, and Mary and I were just plain worn down. Lauren and Kevin were exhausted too, and looked it; Kevin seemed to have barely enough energy to blink. Mark, all of four years old, had recently been ill and looked pale and out of sorts. Haset, who had been home with her new family for about three months now, and who was still less than a year old, seemed fine.

Nati was excited to see Haset again and began shouting, "HELLO, BABY," to her over and over. Mary and I cringed, thinking Nati's shouting would make the baby cry, but unbelievably, young as she was, Haset seemed to recognize Nati. She smiled at him and cooed and we all watched as Nati played with her.

Mary and I had never seen Nati get a chance to interact with a baby before, so we were surprised to see how good Nati was with Haset, but we were not nearly as amazed as our friends seemed to be.

"She's smiling," Lauren said to Kevin.

Kevin shook his head; he, too, was amazed to see his new daughter looking so happy.

"She doesn't usually smile?" I asked.

"Well," Lauren explained, "she's been sick a lot. And she throws up a lot. So, no, not really."

I thought about how Kevin and Lauren had asked me to do a quick medical check on their daughter when I'd seen her in the orphanage and started to feel a bit nervous. I'm not a doctor, but I'd figured that if there had been any really big problems I might have noticed them. "How often does she throw up?" I asked.

Before Lauren could answer me, Nati's eyes grew wide.

"HASET . . . HASET," he said in his very loudest voice.

"Nati, please don't shout," I told him.

"HASET . . . HASET," Nati shouted. He began moving his hands from his stomach into the air. "Haset, always . . ." He stuck his tongue out and pretended to vomit.

"Haset threw up in Ethiopia?" I asked, in a very, very quiet voice.

"SO MUCH THREW UP," Nati said, nodding his head happily. He was clearly thrilled to be able to tell us just how often Haset had been ill back at the orphanage. "So much. Every day. Always, always."

I made a mental note to pay for Kevin's and Lauren's dinner.

We waited for our food to come.

I was hungry. I'm sure I wasn't as hungry as Nati, however, since he hadn't eaten much of anything for, well, a few months actually.

No. Really. A few months.

Before I had kids, I used to think that the phrase *the miracle of life* had something to do with babies and creation and how sweet little toddlers magically grow up and become tax attorneys. Now, however, I know that I was wrong. The true miracle of life is how young children can survive their own weirdness when it comes to food. We've all seen it. Some kids will eat only peanut butter sandwiches for dinner, night after night. Others think anything but plain pasta is disgusting. You want to experience the magic of creation? Then explain to me how one of my daughter's friends lived for two entire years on nothing but rice, milk, and Hershey's kisses. How is that possible?

Nati was more extreme than most kids.

When Nati came here, he wouldn't eat beef. Or pasta. Or rice. Or vegetables, chicken, lamb, fish, most any fruit, candy, or beverage. Nati ate, and would only eat, French fries and bananas. That's it. Though to be fair, he did sometimes combine the two and make banana sandwiches using French fries as the bread. He'd pinch the two fries between his fingers and use them to scoop up a slice of banana and then pop the whole sloppy thing in his mouth as Mary and I groaned.

Nati grew anyway. Still, it just felt . . . wrong. He was just so stubborn in his refusal to even consider eating anything other than those two foods that I could not stop trying to persuade him. Surely he could at least try . . . pizza? Wouldn't he at least like a hamburger? Really, what kid doesn't love pizza? How hard would it be just to try it? Nati, however, was unyielding. He would eat only what he wanted and he refused to try anything he didn't feel like trying. He was unreasonable, pigheaded, and obstinate. What I never considered was the idea that he was also right. After all, it's the job of a parent to turn his or her children into adults. It doesn't work the other way around.

And so each night we'd try to force him to eat something. At mealtimes, Mary and I would put the best food we could in front of him and tell him he had to eat. We tried this with chicken and steak and everything else we could think of, and every night, we'd fight. But Nati is the most determined and stubborn human being I've ever met (come to think of it, most kids are, aren't they?), so before long, we'd give up on making him try different foods and just give him French fries and bananas again. And even then, we'd struggle to get him to eat that one token bite. Mostly it seemed like he was being, well, childish about the whole thing, refusing to eat a tiny bite of food and all. And each time he did eat, he'd do that same weird thing, grabbing one small bit of whatever was on his plate, between two ripped-up pieces of bread or a pair of French fries. No fork. And definitely no chicken, steak, fish, or vegetables.

So we sat and waited for our food, all of us, too tired and dazed to really speak. Now and again, Nati looked up from his plate to smile at Haset and then tell us again just how often she used to throw up. Now and again, Kevin or Lauren would look up from being dazed and, without smiling, confirm that this was, in fact, quite true; their daughter, it seemed, was a veritable fountain, a fact which I had somehow missed. Silly me; it had just never occurred to me to consult on Haset's health records with Dr. Nati that day back in Addis Ababa. And it wasn't just because we weren't speaking the same language when we met. Honestly, it never would have occurred to me that Nati, the kid with the string hanging from his chin, would have been the source of so much medical information. Who knew?

I almost didn't notice when the food came. Not because I

was distracted, but because, well, because Ethiopian food is a little odd. For one thing, it's all served, not with bread in little baskets on the side, like you'd get an Italian restaurant, but actually on top of the bread. The bread, called *injera*, is soft and sort of spongy and functions as a kind of plate for the rest of the food, which is heaped on top of it. Also, there's this other thing about Ethiopian food.

It's disgusting. Or, at least, it was to me that night.

It's mushy, first of all. Seriously mushy. Like someone's already chewed it. That kind of mushy.

All of it looks the mushy same but for the fact that it comes in different colors. There's the yellow mushy stuff, made from some vegetable; the brown mushy stuff, made from lamb; the green mushy stuff, made from either a vegetable or a sickly lamb; and so on. There's spicy mushy stuff, extra-spicy mushy stuff, and not-that-spicy mushy stuff, which is specially prepared for people like me who prefer their mushy stuff not to be painful to consume. All of it looks like slightly lumpy baby food but tastes much, much worse.

The *injera* the food is poured on is sour, like milk that's gone bad. Spongy, gray, sour-milk bread. Yum.

We stared at our plates for a bit. Clay and Grace and our friends' son, Mark, were not especially enthusiastic. Personally, looking at that weird gloppy mess, I felt like crying. I wanted to just put my head down on the table and scream. I wanted to scream about not knowing how sick my friends' baby had been in Ethiopia; I wanted to scream with exhaustion from all the extra work having three kids entailed. I wanted to stomp my feet and cry and just give the hell up because I was so tired and overwhelmed and I certainly didn't want to eat all that slop someone had just tossed in front of me. Nohow. No way.

And then I looked at Nati.

Nati was smiling like a lottery winner. Nati was beaming from ear to ear, cooing at Haset, and shoving mouthfuls of mushy gloppy food into his mouth like the single-most happy person on the planet.

And of course, he was eating his dinner the right way.

Ethiopians put their dinners on top of the bread, because they use the bread like a fork. They pinch a piece of it from the whole, then, holding it between their forefinger and thumb, they scoop some of the meal into the small piece of bread, making a tiny, bite-sized sandwich for themselves. With every bite they eat, there's less and less *injera*, so that at the end of the meal, the plate has been eaten along with the dinner. Everyone eats from the same big helping and at the end of the night, you have no dishes or forks to clean. Brilliant, really. (Okay, I should probably mention here that yes, Ethiopian restaurants do provide forks and plates and yes, those things are common in Ethiopia too. But when Nati ate Ethiopian food, it was strictly a no-fork, no-plate, no-cleaning sort of experience.)

And so Nati sat and ate, the way he'd been taught to eat. He pinched off little mushy green bite-sized sandwiches and little mushy yellow bite-sized sandwiches and he even ate a whole bunch of little mushy brown bite-sized sandwiches. He ate everything on his plate, including, literally, the plate itself, while I sat sullenly, with a fork in my hand, refusing to eat a thing.

In my defense, it didn't take me the entire night to figure a few things out. Halfway through the meal, for instance, I started to realize that all of the food I'd been serving Nati looked pretty much like all of the food that had been served to me that night. Or, at least, that's how all the food I'd served him had looked like to him. I realized that making tiny sandwiches using two French fries and a mushed-up banana was a perfectly normal thing to do. It was certainly the closest thing to a normal thing that Nati could figure out to do. Nati, it turned out, had been doing what he'd been taught to do, all along.

I got the lesson. And luckily for me, because our circumstances were so extreme, the lessons kept coming.

We were at a party not too long after the Ethiopian dinner. Nati still wasn't eating much at that point, but we were getting better at letting him find his own way. (And far, far more important, Haset is now a healthy, wonderful girl who is beautiful in every way.)

It was a birthday party. Nati had been with us about four

months; it was the first real American birthday party that he'd ever attended. And we almost didn't get through the door.

On the way to the party, Nati had been chattering and laughing and being his usual self. We'd had to do some explaining that the gift we were holding was for the birthday boy and not for him, but that this was pretty standard. It was a pretty day and we were all happy and content and looking forward to having fun.

And then, just as we got to the front door, Nati refused to move.

Would not move.

Could not move.

He was, for some reason, terrified.

I tried to prod him along.

Nothing.

I tried to talk to him. His English was pretty good at that point, so I crouched down and tried to explain that Mom and I would be there and that there would be lots of games and fun, and I might just as well have stood there and said, "blah, blah, blah," like Charlie Brown's teacher used to do in the *Peanuts* cartoons, because he wasn't hearing a word of what I was saying.

Normally, that would have been the moment when I began getting upset. I'd been looking forward to Nati getting to run around and play with some kids while Mary and I could relax and just talk to other parents. Normally, I would have just thought Nati was being stubborn by not letting me do what I wanted to do. I would have felt that way except I could see what Nati was seeing.

Literally.

Nati was staring at a tree in the front yard where the party was being held. He barely seemed to blink.

And for good reason. Because there was a tree by the front door and on that tree, dangling from a branch, was a statue of me, his dad, hanging by a rope.

It was totally bizarre and more than a little sinister.

Except that it wasn't. Not even a little.

Okay. Remember how I said that ten years ago I looked like Harry Potter? Yeah, the statue of me, dangling by the rope . . . it was of Harry Potter. Same basic haircut that I had, same glasses. Only this was a piñata. A piñata that looked like a crude version of me. Which, as you can guess, was pretty confusing to my son, who'd never seen a piñata of any kind, let alone a piñata of his father hanging on a tree by a rope.

I can't remember quite how I explained that the statue wasn't me, but somehow I did. I laughed about it and made Nati laugh about it and before too long, Nati decided it was just another strange thing in a place that had almost nothing but strange things.

Then, a little while later, he started to look very anxious when a group of boys his age began to attack the statue of his father with baseball bats.

Yeah, that was sort of tricky. He leaned against me, glancing up at my face to see if I was at all bothered by this weird ritual. Fortunately, one of the first kids up was a pretty good baseball player. When the candy began pouring out of me, wait . . . sorry, when the candy began pouring out of the Harry Potter piñata that looked like me, Nati really didn't know quite what to think. Panic, by that time, had turned into cheerful confusion. And Nati, being Nati, quickly figured out that if parties in his new country were going to include moments where kids smashed statues of his dad with bats, that was going to be just fine with him so long as candy came out when they were done. And I had, once again, gotten a vivid demonstration about perspective. When Nati thought there was a statue of me hanging by a rope, he'd become anxious and hadn't wanted to go in. Then, once he'd figured out that kids bashing the statue of his father with baseball bats meant free candy, he felt better. Okay, it's not a perfect story about perspective. Honestly, it's pretty disturbing, and, in case you're wondering, yes I have encouraged Nati to play soccer instead of baseball, but that's another story for another time.

I knew about perspective. Everyone does. You don't know another man until you've walked a thousand miles in his moccasins and all that. The thing is, when it comes to your kids, they can be just so damn crazy about so much stuff that sometimes it's almost impossible to pause, breathe, and see how they see things. When a kid isn't eating anything but French fries and bananas, when you can't get him to even try pizza or hamburgers, things you know, absolutely know that he'll like, thinking "Well, maybe he has his reasons" takes an almost ridiculous amount of effort. And so we yell and beg and demand that he take just one bite for the love of Pete and he digs in his heels and then suddenly you look up and you notice that you've lost six months of your life to the goofiest stalemate you could ever hope to have.

But sometimes it takes the most extreme situations to bring clarity. I had been willing (though only on my best days) to try to tolerate his craziness. I had been willing now and again to say to myself, "Well, he's having a hard time adjusting," or "Well, kids are like that," but what I hadn't ever imagined was that in his own way, from his own perspective, Nati could be *right*. I mean, I got that I might have to be tolerant, but you only need to be patient and tolerant when other people are wrong. It had never occurred to me that Nati might actually be the one who was right. All of our food was weird and strange-looking and not to be trusted, except, maybe, just maybe, the small, slightly familiar-looking mini sandwiches you could make out of French fries and bananas. And he'd been taught to eat with his hands most of his life. Certainly, to me, all of *his* food felt weird and strange-looking and not to be trusted. If I'd been plucked into a family of Ethiopians, I'd have refused everything but bananas too. And Nati had actually been pretty reasonable when he'd dug his heels in and refused to go to a party where they'd hung his father in effigy.

For some reason, every time Nati refused to eat, I felt

like he was refusing *at* me. I was so caught up in seeing things only from my own perspective that I somehow had convinced myself that Nati was behaving as he was just to drive me crazy. Now, years later, I cherish the advice a friend gave me when he said, "Don't take anything personally. Even if it's meant that way."

Trying to see the world as my kids see it allows me to avoid all sorts of unnecessary righteous anger. More important, unless I force myself into my kids' perspective, I run the risk of spending much of my life coming up with the right answers to the wrong questions.

How? Sometimes it's sort of obvious. At least in retrospect.

Like the way that for three months, when she was five, my daughter's socks were funny.

Not "ha-ha" funny. Funny as in they felt funny. Funny as in we couldn't go to school because her socks felt funny. The not-so-amusing kind of funny. Every day. For three months.

We'd have breakfast. We'd brush our teeth. We'd decide on an outfit for the day. She'd get dressed. And then she'd weep. Because her socks were funny. Every day, every morning, hysteria was served up in my house along with cereal and orange juice. Grace was miserable. I was miserable. Everyone in the house was miserable. At times, Grace and I both expressed our misery so well and so often and so loudly that the neighbors started to become miserable. It was, wait for it . . . miserable.

CLAUDE KNOBLER

HERE ARE THE THINGS I DID TO TRY TO SOLVE
THE PROBLEM IN THE ORDER I TRIED THEM.

1. I tried to adjust Grace's socks. (Hey, I've got nothing against obvious solutions. Sometimes they even work.)
2. I tried adjusting Grace's shoes.
3. I bought Grace new socks.
4. I bought Grace new shoes.
5. I yelled at Grace. (Again, it was worth a shot.) I told Grace that: There. Was. Not. A. Single. Damn. Thing. That. Was. Funny. About. Her. Damn. Socks.
6. I tried, in vain, to reason with Grace to convince her that her socks were fine. That there was nothing wrong with her socks. Or her shoes. Or her feet.
7. I went out one afternoon and had a chocolate chip cookie. By myself.
8. Later that same day, feeling much calmer, I began talking to Grace about all of the hard things in school. We talked about how noisy lunches could be and about how big some of the first-graders she was meeting were. We talked about what girls in her class were wearing and how they looked.

And that was when Grace's socks stopped being funny. Because when I paused, took a breath, and had that chocolate chip cookie, I saw what I hadn't been seeing. Kindergarten was hard. Not so much for me. I'm pretty sure I'd be a straight-A student in any grade up till third, but for my then–five-year-old daughter, kindergarten was hard. You had to do really tough things like color inside the lines and remember where your cubby was. There were all sorts of stressful things, like whether other kids were eating Oreos in their lunches and not being as good at sounding out words as someone else. It's easy to minimize problems when they're not your problems. I'm sure the guy who fixes my car thinks I get way too stressed about something that's as big a no-brainer as why my engine light keeps flashing, because he understands cars, but to me, that stuff can be pretty confusing.

I'd spent a good long time arguing over socks because in my heart of hearts, I simply couldn't accept not just that Grace was having a hard time, but that having a hard time in kindergarten was perfectly reasonable. One day, when Clay was four, I asked him how his day at preschool had been. He said, "It was okay, but sometimes all the climbing and block building gets kind of hard." I thought that was cute and funny and, you know, kind of ridiculous, but the truth is, when you're four, all that climbing and block building does get kind of hard. You're four. Climbing two feet in the air is scary. Building something and then having it topple over is stressful.

And because I couldn't or wouldn't see things from my daughter's perspective, I kept coming up with the right answers to the wrong questions. When I thought the problem was Grace's socks, my problem was where to buy better socks. When I thought the problem was Grace's shoes, my problem was where to buy better shoes. And when I thought the problem was that Grace was freaking out for no reason at all, my problem was how to change her behavior by yelling at her into being sane. It was only when I realized that she was honestly and legitimately having a hard time that the right answer to the right question appeared. I looked at my overwhelmed five-year-old daughter and began to sympathize instead of condescend, and help her express her fears. And then her socks stopped making us both crazy.

Just as important, the longer I focused on the symptom, which was Grace's behavior, the bigger the problem got. Attention is a magnifying glass. What you focus on gets larger. The more we talked about Grace's socks, the worse that problem got. So we talked about other things. Casually. We talked about the good parts about kindergarten and the bad parts. As I discovered things that Grace liked about school, I began to talk about those things before she could have her regular morning meltdown. And when she wanted to talk about things she was struggling with, I listened.

All of which, by the way, would be a beautiful, touching story about what an enlightened parent I was and am, were it not for the fact that it took me three months to figure all that out. I kind of got stuck between #5 and #6 and just kept

yelling at Grace over and over. Not my best moments, to be sure. And a quick word about yelling and perspective. Take a thirty-five-year-old man who's five feet nine and weighs 145 pounds. He has a four-year-old daughter who's a bit over three feet tall and weighs 40 pounds. In order to understand what it feels like to that child when his father yells at her, imagine that father being yelled at by a 640-pound, eight-foot-six-inch man. Oh, and that man, the 640-pound one, is also the only person who brings him food. Just something for me to keep in mind. (Note to any reader with a calculator and a tiny bit of math skills: Please feel free to change the ratios.)

The thing that kept me stuck between #5 and #6, the

thing that kept me gritting my teeth and trying not to yell, was the fear that haunts parents all the time. What if they stay that way?

Most of the really bad parenting I've done in my life has been done in the self-righteous name of "Making Sure They Don't Grow Up That Way." And so as Grace cried and whined, I became determined to Raise A Strong Young Woman. Which is fine, really it is, except, like all behavior dictated by fear, it was also a little crazy. Kids really don't need discipline or a stern talking-to in order to grow out of being children. It happens kind of sort of on its own.

When Clay was five I was convinced he was just like me . . . and not in a good way. One day, I was telling a friend that I was sure that Clay would wind up with all sorts of troubles. He was too sensitive, just like me. He didn't handle change well, just like me. He got anxious over things he could have just ignored, just like me. My son was clearly destined to wind up with every single problem I'd ever gone through and would clearly need all sorts of help in the years to come.

My friend listened to me for a while and then pointed something out. "You know," he told me, "Clay is five. He's supposed to act that way. Your only problem is you're still trying to outgrow that stuff."

Happily, he was right. Clay is no longer five. He drives, he shaves, he handles change like a pro, and he worries only as much as he needs to and not a drop more. The notion that I needed to drag him into emotional maturity turned out to have been nothing more than a product of my own lack of emotional maturity. He did not need to learn how to be more mature any more than I needed to teach him how to get taller. It just sort of happened. When I grit my teeth and decide that I'm going to fix my kids before they grow up to be the wrong kind of adult, I'm really trying to solve a problem that hasn't happened yet and may never happen at all. Likewise, my attempts to make sure that Grace stopped whining so she could grow up to be a strong, independent woman who didn't depend on unreliable men to take care of her, were, well, yeah, pretty nutty.

When I trust that my point of view is the only correct way of seeing, I tend to make all sorts of mistakes. It's almost impossible not to.

Take Nati's first real basketball game.

Clay was seven, and his friend Gage was six. Somehow, Gage had found out about the NBA and had become consumed with that one thing in the way that kids sometimes do. So when Gage discovered that Clay was about to get a new brother all the way from Africa, he was beyond excited. Because Gage ate, dreamed, played, and talked basketball twenty-four hours a day, seven days a week, he'd noticed that most of the players on his favorite teams were not short Jewish guys like him, but rather, tall black men, as he assumed Nati would be. Basically Gage didn't think Clay's family was adopting a child, he thought we were getting a great draft pick for our team.

I suppose this would be a good point to state the obvious. Nati came here never having played basketball and knowing nothing of the game. He's a good athlete but not superhuman. Gage knew none of that, though, when he first met Nati, and so when after he and his mom, Nancy, and Clay, Grace, Nati, Mary, and I had dinner one summer night I suggested that we could play some basketball, he was enthusiastic. We'd been eating at his grandmother's apartment complex, and since the basketball court there was empty, we decided to play a full-court game; Clay and Gage versus Nati and me. Gage was thrilled.

Before long, we fell into a small routine. Gage and Clay would dribble the ball quickly, pass, and then take a shot. After the shot had gone in, I'd take the ball and pass it to Nati, who then carried the ball in his arms while running as fast as he could to the half-court line. Then he'd toss the ball to me and say, "Go, Dad, you go," indicating that I was now expected to go and shoot for our team.

When my shots missed, Nati would take it badly. First he'd fall to his knees, and then he'd lie facedown on the court saying, "Nooooo," until Gage or Clay dribbled by him. When I made the shot, he was thrilled. I'd point at him and he, while running backward to defend, would hold his hand out. I'd then give him a high five; he, in turn, would slap the back of my hand, and then we'd both make a fist and bang our hands together. We didn't score much, but when we did, we celebrated in style.

Clearly, the game was an unusual one. Nati never dribbled, he frequently ran off the court onto a nearby patio area in order to lose his defender, and he never crossed the half-court line. Then, it got weirder.

Gage was dribbling the ball downcourt when Nati ran toward him and began hugging him. I sighed. In the short time he'd been with us, I had already seen that Nati sometimes got in other kids' faces when he wanted to be liked. He hugged kids who might not want to be hugged and didn't always seem to understand people's need for a bit of space. I felt myself well up with concern about his future. I worried that perhaps we'd adopted a child who would never quite fit in. I worried about how Nati would do in school. I worried that other kids would think he was weird, that he'd be made fun of, that he would never learn to have an American sense of personal space and boundaries.

Because I was worried about Nati and his future, I slowed down as I dribbled the ball and shouted to Nati that hugging wasn't okay right now. Nati shook his head. I began to lose my temper. My fear and perspective were making it clear that it was time for me to teach Nati that he couldn't just hug kids randomly. It was time to make sure he didn't grow up to be the weird kid no one wanted to play with.

"Nati," I said, this time in a sterner voice, "you have to listen to me. You can't hug the other players in the middle of a basketball game. You have to stop that."

Gage was looking at Nati now, and I could sense his disappointment. He'd finally gotten to play basketball with someone who was lucky enough to look like one of his heroes, and here the kid was hugging him in the middle of a game. I told Nati to stop again, but again he shook his head.

I was still standing just shy of midcourt, absentmindedly dribbling the ball.

"I'm sorry, Gage," I said, "he's learning."

Gage shrugged, and I dribbled over closer to where he was standing, with Nati still draped onto him.

"Nati, let go of Gage," I said. He didn't, though. Instead he shook his head, and so I got ready to use my "mean dad" voice. The one that says, *Do it because I'm your father and I'm big and I want it done now.*

Nati was still shaking his head no. Now I was angry about his defiance as well as his behavior. Over the years I've found that I generally know when I'm about to lose my temper. There's a moment when I almost decide, yes, I'm going to yell, because dammit, that's what needs to happen. These kids must learn and yelling is the only thing that will get through to them. I was just about ready to do that.

And then I looked again. I looked again at my son who didn't quite know the rules of basketball, but who had certainly figured something out. And then it hit me.

Nati wasn't shaking his head no, he was shaking his head "go." As in, "Dribble, you idiot, I've finally figured out how to cover this guy." And then I realized Nati wasn't hugging Gage; he was guarding him by pretending to hug him. You don't see that move much in pro games, but honestly, it's pretty hard to defend against. And so I dribbled right past Gage to the basket. Clay, who'd been just waiting quietly for me to deal with Nati, got it just after I did; he chased after me, but it was too late. The ball went in, Nati and I did our high fives, and that was that.

Of course, it's not always that simple.

Which brings me to the whole raising-teenagers thing.

I have three teenagers now. Clay, just seven when Nati first came, is eighteen, a high school senior, and ready to go to college. Grace and Nati are both in the thick of their teenage years. (I like to call them "the twins." For reasons I can't understand, the nickname hasn't really caught on with either of them yet. But I'm still trying.)

There's no question that the problems teenagers get into are significantly more serious than the problems you have with young children. Drugs, food issues, troubled relationships; really anything short of them turning into vampires and roaming the night skies is pretty much on the table. So what's the secret?

It's all the same.

Let's start with the normal, average, run-of-the-mill chaos.

There's a lot of normal, average, run-of-the-mill chaos.

To start with, all three of my kids' rooms are disgusting. Genuinely and honestly disgusting. Nati, who used to not eat anything, now seems to be running a disreputable cafeteria out of his bedroom. There are often dirty plates and half-eaten boxes of cookies on his bedside table. Dirty clothes are everywhere but the hamper. Wet towels are on the floor.

His room is the clean one.

As millions of other parents have learned, there's really only one way of dealing with a teenager who won't clean their room, and that's to make sure you turn your head away when you're shutting their door in the morning after they leave for school. There is, however, a trick to staying happy while you ignore the normal, daily chaos: the chores that don't get done, the filth that piles up, and the way your kids refuse to tell you that they've signed you up to bring a choco- late cake to their class breakfast, to which you are not invited, until the morning of said breakfast. That trick is the differ- ence between tolerating your life and something a lot closer to happiness.

Perspective.

Every day I have to remember that meal I had with Nati in that Ethiopian restaurant and remind myself that if I'm going to be happy today, I'm going to have to remember to eat through my son's eyes. Though I try not to use that phrase before breakfast. Or out loud.

What makes perspective truly difficult is understanding that you might be wrong. Most of the time, I operate under the assumption that if what I believed was wrong, I'd believe something else. I don't think of myself as the smartest man on the planet . . . it's just that I assume whatever I'm thinking at any given moment must be right. So it's easy for me to feel like my kids have it easy, what with not having to pay rent or bills. And then, when I remember all that mushy food that Nati wouldn't eat, I pause, catch my breath, and remember that I have friends and acquaintances who are doctors, writers, math teachers, and stay-at-home parents. My friend Piper makes jewelry. My friend Keith is a chef. My friend Kevin is a computer programmer. I have friends who work in real estate, another who is a painter, and another who is a doctor. My wife works in finance, staring at six computer monitors all at once, each of which is filled with information that I don't know anything about.

You know what none of my friends do? All of that.

I do not have a single friend who is a real estate agent and a computer programmer, or who works as a chef and a doctor. Which is good, because I also don't know a single adult who is good at everything. Most of us are good at either writing or math, not both. And yet every day, all three of my teenage kids go off to school, where they must demonstrate competency in writing, art, advanced math, science, and a foreign language. If, God forbid, they show no skill at one of these subjects, if they, for example, fail a few tests in math, then they stay after school for more instruction or get a tutor. They are expected to be at least "good" in everything.

You know what? I'm okay with their rooms being gross. From the moment they open their eyes till the moment when they finish their homework, their lives are structured by other people. They have to study math whether or not they have any aptitude in the subject. They have to read books that they are assigned, even if every reasonable person living on the planet today knows for a fact that *The Scarlet Letter* is an awful, boring book fit to be used only as a paperweight. They have no say in much of anything. Their desire to have total control of their own tiny living space is not really all that unreasonable from that perspective. In fact, it makes sense, even if the result of their choice is that I'm uncomfortable entering their room without a hazmat suit.

I'm not saying kids shouldn't have to study science or poetry. But while not having to pay rent or, you know, raise children, may seem like a life of ease and comfort, that's not always the case. And when I, as a parent, decide that I'm going to make sure that my hardworking children don't grow up to be self-indulgent slobs who expect other people to pick up their dirty clothes . . . well, honestly, I think that's sort of crazy. I do hope that my kids will learn to put their dirty socks in, on, or near a laundry hamper. But right now, living as I do in this day, using every bit of perspective I can muster, I think it best to let a whole lot slide.

My kids don't really have a lot of chores. And yet they're not especially spoiled. Yes, they do put away the dishes after dinner, but honestly, there are plenty of nights when I take that over. What I get instead is what I want most for both me today and for them in the future: a sense of kindness, love, and patience with each other. Instead of arguing over each "infraction"—a messy room or an uneaten vegetable left on a plate—I choose instead to try to simply understand their stresses and help them understand mine. When I come into the house with groceries, my kids tend to just get up and help me with them, without it being a job that they have so they can learn to be responsible. I want to help them. They want to help me. When school is especially hard, I help them with their dishes. When I have more than a bag or two to carry into the house, they help me carry the load. We manage to often treat each other with sympathy and gentleness, and those are things you can show your children, not by lecturing them, but by demonstrating them yourself.

The odd thing about the terror you feel as a parent is that it always seems to come to the door disguised as love and good intentions. My mother was terrified, truly terrified, that if she didn't plead, nag, cajole, and beg me to clean my room every day, I would grow up to be an irresponsible slob who'd struggle to hold down a job and whose apartment would forever be home to a nest of fleas and vermin because I'd never learn to wash my dishes or take out the trash. That's not to imply that my mother is crazy, by the way, because the truth is, that's the trajectory I seemed to be on. I was a teenage boy who really was an irresponsible slob . . . just like a whole lot of other teenage boys. My mother, like so many mothers before and after her, believed that it was her job as a parent to cure me of being a teenager.

You know what happened? Life. Life and girls.

I moved out. I started taking out the garbage and it wasn't an especially big deal. I noticed that girls seemed to like me a bit more when they came over on days when my apartment was fairly clean. I grew up. Not because my mother set high standards and demanded that I become a decent human being. I grew up because time passed, I matured, and oh, by the way, I'd had the good fortune to see what decent human beings did. I didn't listen to what my mother said, but I did watch what she did.

Plus, I really, really wanted girls to come over.

That's not to say that my kids do nothing or that I should function as their maid every day. Let me be incredibly clear about that, if only because of the very small chance that my kids may decide to read this book. OF COURSE, YOUR KIDS SHOULD HELP AROUND THE HOUSE. The question isn't what they do, it's why and how they are expected to do it. When I assign my kids chores because *dammit, it's time they learned some responsibility and the world isn't going to take care of them, oh no it's not, and if they think I'm going to do everything for them, well they have another thing coming* . . . things tend not to work out so well. They know why I'm doing what I'm doing and they resent the notion that I think their lives are some kind of fairy-tale paradise.

Which, again, makes sense. One of the things that people crave most is appreciation. Not in the sense of "Oh, what a good job you did," but in the simple acknowledgment that what they did took effort. Telling a teenager who's struggling to decipher Shakespeare's sonnets, calculus, the opposite sex, and AP Spanish that they've got to learn some responsibility is bound to cause hurt feelings. Just as my feelings are often hurt when my kids are thoughtless, as of course they sometimes are. I want them to know that I've worked hard for them and I want them to acknowledge that fact by helping out. Parents have been talking about how their children don't appreciate all that they do for a long, long time, but appreciation has to be a two-way street. And yelling at your kid for not appreciating all you do is a pretty good way of demonstrating that you don't appreciate all that they're doing.

By not making chores into a battleground, by being okay with a messy room, what I've often lucked into are kids who help out not because they have to, but because they're the sorts of people who want to (or who are willing to, even when they don't want to). And maybe they don't seem to clutter up the living room with all of their stuff all that often because they do have an area they can decorate with as much filth as they like. Or maybe it's just that when I'm not desperate to mold them into something, a bit of clutter in my living room doesn't seem all that hard to deal with. I haven't told my kids that they need to learn discipline, and so when I come home with groceries, no battle lines have been drawn. They just . . . bring in the groceries. Because people tend to do that sort of thing when they're not desperate to prove a point. When I don't let my fear that my kids will end up being fired for keeping unwashed plates in their office rule my thoughts, all sorts of wonderful things wind up happening in the here and now. Which is good, because the here and now is where I do most of my living.

The way I see it, I'm trying to raise kind, intelligent, focused, decent human beings capable of achieving both personal and professional success. Or, failing all that, I'm trying to raise three kids who'll make enough money not to have to live in my basement and who will, one day, after they marry, give me grandchildren to play with. With either one of those things as my goal, imposing my perspective on my children can only be counterproductive. I don't want them always looking to me for the answers. I want them to find ways to find their own answers.

I want to set the tone, not just for one conversation, in which my point of view may or may not be the correct one, but for the general course of our time together. I can't do that by demanding that everyone see each situation the same way I see it. That means that constantly begging my kids to be responsible won't work. All they can learn from that is that they might get me off their backs if they pick up their towels, which is not really what responsibility is all about. I can only help them by being as kind, humble, focused, intelligent, and useful as I know how to be (and then simply hope that now and again they're paying attention to me in my good moments).

Of course, there are times that call for, let's say, more dramatic and immediate measures. Years ago my sister, who became a parent before I did, taught me that the most important thing you can do for teenagers is try to keep them alive until their brains come to full maturation, and to that I can only say, "Amen." (Though to be slightly more accurate, I'm pretty sure the exact words she used were more along the lines of "I just want to keep them alive till they're done being crazy.") If your child is texting while driving, I'm all in favor of hiding the car keys and grounding them till they're thirty. If your daughter is sneaking off to meet up with that perfectly delightful older boy who recently got paroled, there's really nothing wrong with pulling up stakes and entering the witness protection program. Assuming, that is, that you've already tried seeing the world through her eyes. While we, as parents, may be dismissive of any relationship conducted between two people who fairly recently were both fetuses, remembering that our children's feelings are real can mean the difference between Juliet sneaking off to see Romeo and at least bringing him home to meet you for the occasional dinner. On the other hand, on the texting-while-driving thing . . . yeah, grounded till thirty.

And yet, same as with treating an illness, the best medicine is what you do to avoid getting sick in the first place. Maybe my son Clay is an irredeemable slob who will never ever learn to put away things he's done with . . . but then again, maybe he's a stressed-out teenager. And if the problem is stress, then my yelling at him about that mess isn't really going to make the problem go away. My yelling at him about papers left all over his floor, when those papers are only the symptom of the larger problem, is really just the right answer to the wrong problem. Because if the real problem isn't that Clay is sloppy, but *is* how can I let my son know that he's going to be fine, that I recognize and appreciate how hard it is to do what he does and that SATs, AP exams, and calculus tests will eventually pass, then the answer is not to yell at him. The answer is to help him feel heard and to give him the right to have some control over his own destiny, or at least of his own room.

I can't really know that I'm right about anything that hasn't happened yet, even the things I feel sure about. I do know one thing, though. Nati managed to learn to eat all sorts of food that I've given him over the years. That problem has taken care of itself, as I should have known it would. Come to think of it, I've even grown to really love Ethiopian food, which no longer seems quite so strange and foreign as it once did. And Nati didn't have to nag me about it a single time. I grew up all on my own.

# LESS THAN PERFECT IS PERFECT ENOUGH

---

*How Not Yelling at My Son*

*for Almost Six Whole Seconds Taught Me*

*It's Okay to Get It All Wrong*

L ET ME TELL YOU A REALLY AWFUL STORY ABOUT MY WIFE. It's a horrible story, really and truly awful, so before I begin, I'd like to tell you that I really do love my wife. She is, in spite of the story I'm about to tell, a wonderful woman, wife, and mother. For many years now, she's been the bread-winner in our house and if it weren't for the work she does every day at her office, I would never have been able to write books like this that tell awful, horrible stories that make her look really, really bad.

So again, let me make it very clear to you that I love my wife and that no matter what I'm about to say, I really do hope you will believe me when I tell you that she is an amaz-ing mom.

Okay, here's the awful story.

My wife and I were having a hard time with Nati. We were yelling a lot. We were miserable a lot. Worst of all, we were becoming the sorts of parents that we'd never, ever wanted to be.

If there was one small bit of luck in all that screaming and yelling, it was that we tended in a very unplanned way to al-ternate in our misery. In the wake of the massive change of having added an exuberant, loud, goofy five-year-old boy into our once quiet and peaceful family, Mary and I seemed to take turns struggling with our new life. Whoever's turn it was to panic or become frustrated would inevitably lose their temper with Nati and then, filled with remorse and regret, turn to the other and fall apart. Sometimes Mary would come to me feeling overwhelmed or guilty about how she'd lost her cool with Nati. Then, the next week, it would be my turn and I'd come staggering into our room to tell her how hard I was finding it to be the sort of father I wanted to be. Still, pretty much every day, either Mary or I was struggling with our new son.

He was just so determined. He wanted more of everything. He thought nothing we did was good enough. He was louder, needier, and more demanding than anything we'd ever experienced. When we gave him anything, no matter how big or nice, he was not, for a single second, satiated. If we took him to get ice cream, he wanted three scoops instead of two. If we gave him three scoops, he wanted toppings. If we gave him toppings, he wanted a toy. If we gave him three scoops, toppings, and a toy, he wanted to choose which car seat he used on the way home. If we let him choose which car seat he wanted on the way home from having four scoops of ice cream with toppings and a new toy, he wanted to drive the car himself. And when we told him that state law made it impossible for us to let him drive without a license, he told us we were being unfair, argued, and sulked. We simply could not win.

So we said, "No." All the time.

"No, you can't eat the whole cake."

"No, Nati, that's your sister's toy, put it down."

"No, Nati, those are my keys, I need those."

No. No. No.

There's nothing wrong with saying no to your kid, particularly when he's demanding to drive your car. What really bothered me was that we seemed to be angry all the time. We seemed to be yelling all the time. Nati seemed to be forcing us to say no on a constant basis, and our "nos" were getting louder and louder every day.

Mary told me that she felt the same way, and so we decided to give ourselves a challenge.

We decided to see how long we could go without criticizing Nati or yelling at him. Sort of a contest, really.

I looked at my watch. I told Mary the time. We figured if we could go a day or two without losing our tempers, we'd be able to slowly work our way back toward being the calm, rational human beings we could still dimly remember once having been.

Our contest began.

It did not go well for Mary.

Six seconds.

Six seconds is how long my wife lasted. Six seconds, timed on my watch, before she turned to Nati and in an angry, harsh tone shouted at our son, "Nati, no, don't do that!" I don't even remember what the kid was doing: teasing Gracie, playing with a knife, trying to buy a private jet on Amazon . . . no idea, but I do know that my wife lasted just six seconds before she'd shouted "No!"

Do I judge her for that? Hell yes, I do. What kind of awful person can't make it a full minute without criticizing her own child? What kind of awful human being can't go ten seconds without telling an orphan—an *orphan*, for God's sake—that he's misbehaving? It's reprehensible, is what it is.

And I would have told Mary so, had she not beaten me by four seconds.

That's right. Two seconds after I suggested to my wife that we see how long we could go without criticizing Nati or shouting at him, I shouted the word *no*. Two seconds. One, two: NO!

I think it's important here to make sure you know and understand that I'm not exaggerating for effect. Please believe me when I say that I lasted exactly two seconds and not a single second longer than that. When I say I lasted only two seconds before shouting the word *no*, I don't mean two seconds as in, "I'm almost ready, just give me two seconds," or "I'll be downstairs in a couple of seconds." I mean exactly one second plus one second. Two. Seconds.

Do you know how long two seconds are? I'll give you a hint. You can barely say the words *two seconds* in two seconds. It will take you more time to find the second hand on your watch than it will to watch two seconds pass once you do find your second hand.

No, really. Go ahead, count to two. Use *Mississippis* like you did when you were a kid. Count, "one Mississippi, two Mississippi," just to see how little time that is. Count and see . . . what's that? You finished already? Oh, right. Well, two seconds is pretty short, isn't it?

Again, I have no idea what it was that Nati managed to do in two seconds. All I know is I said this:

"Okay, Mary, let's see how long we can go without shouting at Nati. It's seven o'clock. Starting now, we'll—Nati, NO! Put that down—dammit!"

Two seconds and I swear I'm not rounding down.

And that was when I was focused on not yelling at my kid. Those two seconds of restraint were the result of real effort and discipline. I was much, much worse when I wasn't trying.

You may now feel free to judge me. And my wife.

Unless . . .

Unless you've ever yelled at your children at the top of your voice that you wanted some quiet in this house, RIGHT NOW!

I think my personal favorite low point, though, came after Nati threatened Clay. Nati was just being a little brother, trying to get his older brother's attention, when he told Clay that he was going to "get him" if Clay didn't do what he wanted. I can't be certain, but Nati might have even indicated that he'd be pinching, punching, or shoving Clay if his demands weren't met. Clay was taller and stronger than Nati and more than capable of taking care of himself, but because Nati was going through a bit of a stage where he threatened Clay with that stuff quite often, I decided to step in. Well, not so much "decided" as got really angry and started yelling.

"Nati," I told my youngest son, "if you ever threaten Clay again I'm going to knock your block off."

Seriously, I threatened a kid to make sure he'd better stop making threats . . . or else.

And you know what? I have neither shame nor remorse. I have yelled for quiet, threatened in order to put an end to threats, and lasted a mere two seconds in my attempt to avoid yelling at a child. Am I embarrassed? Hardly.

The absolute, unavoidable truth about parenting is this: If you never lose your temper with your child, you are not spending enough time with your child.

You know who doesn't make parenting mistakes? People who are pregnant with their first child. They get everything perfect right up until the kid is actually born. After that, it's right down in the swamp with the rest of us.

Think about babies. Nati didn't come along till he was already five, but I was there the days Clay and Grace were born. They were as perfect as any creature could ever be. I get a pang in my chest when I think about how soft Clay's skin was. I get misty-eyed when I remember how I held Grace in my arms, seconds after she was born, and how I fell so head over heels in love with her in that single moment that one of the nurses in the delivery room actually laughed out loud at me and said, "Looks like some little girl already has her daddy wrapped around her pinky." And it's true, I'd have bought her a car that very day if she could have found the words to ask for one.

And I wouldn't go back to my kids being babies if you paid me.

Babies are brutally hard work. You know how I know that? I know that because the conversations I most remember having with my wife, with the other parents I knew, and with complete and total strangers who saw me with my kids when they were babies were all about naps.

Children who napped every afternoon were referred to, without fail, as "good babies." Good babies slept all through the night, of course, but also somehow managed to sleep late in the mornings, too. People who had babies who napped twice a day every day were treated like *gods* by other parents. We clamored for their secrets. By what magic spell or elixir were they able to get their child to go down for naps with such ease? The single great personal trait you could hope for in your infant was a temporary case of narcolepsy that would heal of its own accord as soon as your kid was old enough to enter preschool.

You think that's a coincidence? Sure, babies are the single most adorable things on the planet, but have you ever seen anyone hope that they'd get the chance to sit next to one on a cross-country flight?

When Clay was just under a year old, I took him to the shopping mall. He wasn't any more interested in shopping than I was, but he hadn't napped and I was tired and bored and thought I'd at least like to glance into store windows as I pushed him in his stroller praying he'd go to sleep. As I trudged, a sweet, silver-haired old lady smiled her best sweet smile, cooed at my son, and then said to me, "Enjoy these days. They're the best days of your life."

Without pausing or breaking stride, I looked at that sweet, lovely old woman and said, "Then shoot me now," and kept on walking.

A baby will scream at the top of their surprisingly strong

lungs directly into your ear until you give them precisely what they want, without ever telling you what they want. Honestly, who does that?

Toddlers? Adorable. My daughter used to dress up like Disney princesses and I'd carry her in my arms and she'd kiss my face. Heaven. And brutally hard.

In the entire history of the spoken word, no one has ever said "You are so childish!" and meant it as a good thing. When my kids were very young I made the mistake of going on the occasional beach vacation with them. I played with them in the pool, I watched them jump into the water, I got them snacks and put sunscreen on them, I took them to the bathroom when they needed to go (which seemed to be every five minutes), and played games with them in the sun nonstop. Then, when I was ready to check out and go home, I realized I'd been on vacation for only an hour and a half. Yes, that was me you saw weeping by the pool that time. Got a problem with that?

Children are hard and there's no way you can be with them on a full-time basis and not occasionally stumble into trouble. When Nati had been here a year, he took an interest in sports, by which I mean, he took an interest in sitting next to me and Clay while we watched sports and rooting against whichever team we were rooting for. One day, Clay and I were snuggled up together on the couch watching a football game. Nati asked us which team we liked. By this time, Nati had been with us long enough so that we knew what he was up to. And so I tricked my son, a newcomer to American sports teams, into believing that Clay and I were rooting *against* the players in the striped uniforms, whom I called the "zebra guys." Nati, ever the perfect little brother, began rooting *for* the zebra guys.

And yes, the "zebra guys" were the referees. Clay and I quietly watched our game while Nati tried to annoy us by saying, "Yay, zebra guys!" over and over. Am I proud of that? Well, actually on that one, a bit. Still, it wasn't exactly perfect parenting. But then, such a thing doesn't really exist.

If I have learned anything about how to parent, it's only because I've spent so much time seeing what doesn't work. In part, my many missteps were because Nati was so intent on provoking me and challenging me as often as possible. On the other hand, going from two kids to three is a huge change, no matter who that third kid may be. Suddenly, kids outnumber parents, which means that no matter how good a parent you are being with whichever kid you're spending time with at that moment, someone in your family will always, always, always feel left out. Often they will actually be left out. There's more of them than there are of you, and there's really not much you can do to outsmart math.

Still, I tried. I tried shouting at Nati. I tried setting limits and being strict and giving him consequences and time-outs. For me, the most frustrating times were when I'd punish Nati only to find that he'd refuse to be unhappy. If I told him he couldn't watch TV to punish him because of the way he'd teased his brother or sister, he'd plaster a big smile on his face and start making himself an elaborate lunch in the kitchen, till the noise and mess made me nostalgically long for the time, only a short while before, when he'd been sitting quietly in front of the TV and only annoying his sibling during the commercials.

To this day, on those rare occasions when I do feel the need to do anything approaching a traditional punishment for my kids, I prefer finding ways to punish them that will make my life better. I have on occasion punished Nati by refusing to allow him to go to a party that I'd have to pick him up from late at night. I don't know that he learns anything, but I do know that I wind up getting to go to sleep at an early hour. When a kid is bugging me, I'm always ready to say that he can't have friends over, and never ever willing to say that he can't go and hang out at his friend's house. "Every parent for themself" is my motto.

Which is all just a way of saying that one more thing I learned I'd have to let go of once I had three kids, in addition to the idea that I was going to be the single-handed molder of their characters and destinies, was my preconceptions about what being a "good" parent would look like. Even as I sit here, literally writing the book (or at least *a* book) about parenting, I know that I have provided each of my kids with ample material for a lifetime of therapy sessions. I have had more arguments with Nati than I can count, often about trivial non-sense that neither of us really cares about. None of that means that I'm doing my job as a parent incorrectly.

It is impossible, for example, to raise a teenager, let alone three of them, without realizing that sometimes kids need to argue in order to separate themselves from you and become autonomous individuals. (And yes, the term *autonomous individuals* does sort of mean "jerks." Or at least, acting like a jerk can be a pit stop on the way to becoming an autonomous individual.) They will, in order to achieve some kind of separation, twist your words, sulk over trivial slights, and behave in any number of unreasonable ways all in order to get you to be angry enough at them so that they can find out that it's safe to storm off away from you. No amount of being kind, rational, or loving will stop those interactions from becoming arguments because the whole point of the interaction is to have an argument. Nati likes to argue and will, if necessary, do so even when you agree with him. Clay has the occasional stress-induced blowup.

There are times when kids need to fight with their parents, when nothing you do is right and everything you do bothers them. Accepting the inevitable conflicts is the first step I can take toward making those conflicts more bearable. Allowing yourself to be a bad parent turns out to be a pretty good way of being a good one. The goal again, for me, is to simply aim for less conflict, less worry, and less stress. Yes, I can frequently do that by trusting in the overall tone I set in the house by my own behavior, but sometimes I can also do that by accepting that sometimes my kids and I will drive each other a little crazy.

When I'm at fault, I try to admit it and apologize. I can't really remember my father ever apologizing to me when I grew up, but then, raising Nati quickly made it clear to me that not apologizing wasn't going to be an option. One day, early on, when I'd shouted at Nati to be quiet or to stop jumping or doing whatever it was that day that was making me crazy and panicked and worried that we'd bitten off way more than we could chew, Clay looked up at me and said, "Dad, he's only been here for like a month . . . from Africa! It's not his fault if he doesn't know what to do yet."

"Right, right," I muttered. "Only a month? I forgot." And so I'd find Nati and apologize for losing my cool. Apologizing for losing my temper instead of just focusing on what Nati had done to cause me to lose my temper sometimes felt like a display of weakness. But if conflict is inevitable, if arguments are natural, if being a parent is just plain so hard that it's impossible to do it without sometimes doing it badly, then there are bound to be times when the best I can hope to do as a parent is show my children how to clean up after their emotional messes by cleaning up after my own. If my goal is to win every fight, I'm in for a world of suffering and misery. If my goal, on the other hand, is to avoid the fights I can avoid and cheerfully endure the ones I can't, all while showing my kids through my own actions how to behave after they're done behaving badly, well, then I have a chance to live sanely and happily. Or, you know, as close to that as you can get when you have three kids. The trick for me is to remember that I don't need to win every fight. I just need to acknowledge that I will be having fights and that the best thing I can do is move on from them as quickly and gracefully as possible.

Most of all, though, I carry with me the great wisdom passed down to me from the generations: When you are truly angry, you should always stop, breathe, and count to nearly two. Works almost every time.

# EVERYTHING BAD IS EVERYTHING GOOD

*How the Sound of Thirty*

*Kindergarteners Chanting Taught Me*

*Context Is Everything*

CHANTING.

I'd had an idea of what Nati's first birthday party might be like. I'd thought about how excited he'd be about getting lots of presents for the first time ever. I'd wondered how many kids in his class would want to come. I'd pictured the cake and the way Nati would run around feeling excited. The chanting, though . . . well, that really threw me. A lot.

When I was a kid, you had to fit in to be popular. I wore Converse sneakers to school because that's what my friends did. Had they worn a different kind of sneaker to school, I would have worn those. I didn't much care about footwear; I just sort of followed the crowd. The thing of it is, though, I'm a follower at heart because it never occurred to me, not as a child or an adult, that someone had to decide what was cool for there to be a cool thing to copy. I mean, some kid had to have decided that he liked Converse sneakers, right?

Which brings me to Nati's first friend in America, Augie.

Nati met Augie at summer camp and for whatever reason, they clicked. Both of them were five, so language wasn't too big a barrier. They liked running in dirt, farting, and throwing grapes, which is as good a foundation for a friendship as any. I'd watch the two of them and always felt insanely happy as they laughed together. "Look at that," I thought to myself, "Nati's fitting in. He's learning how to be a kid here."

I was very nearly right about that, too.

One day, I spoke to Augie's father. I introduced myself and he, of course, asked how Nati was doing. I said that he seemed to be getting along pretty well, and that he was starting to fit in. I told him how glad I was that Augie and Nati were playing so well and how grateful I was that Augie was being so kind with Nati. He smiled and said that Augie really liked Nati. In fact, he went on to say just that morning his son had woken up and told him, "Dad, Augie *shent*." He'd had no idea what his son was saying to him, of course, until Augie explained that Nati had taught him the Amharic word for "pee."

As they drove to camp, Augie had filled his father in on all the other words he'd learned from Nati. Neither Augie's dad nor I could recall what the Amharic word for "fart" is, but Nati had taught it to Augie, and wouldn't you know it, it turns out that knowing how they say all sorts of things in Ethiopia was pretty cool to the other kids at camp here in the United States.

The chanting, though, I definitely did not see coming.

When Nati first went to school, he got off to a rocky beginning. For starters, he kept escaping.

One day in class, Nati got bored. So he left. When the teachers realized he was gone, they panicked and began hunting for him. They checked the halls and the bathroom, only to find that Nati had just gone out to the yard to play on the jungle gym all by himself. His teachers told him his class was inside working. Nati did what he does when he gets caught doing something wrong: He smiled and then said, as if he'd just remembered something, "Oh . . . yeah."

But Nati was cute, he didn't speak much English, and of course so many things were new to him then. His teacher didn't think much of it.

Until he snuck out a second time. The same day.

Once again, his teacher looked up from the chaos of twenty-four kids. The school Nati attended grouped kids from kindergarten to second grade, ages five to eight, so there was a lot going on in that room. When Nati's teacher realized Nati was gone again, she was a bit less panicked. She started her search for him at the jungle gym, and that's where she found him.

"Nati," his teacher told him, "we're inside now. You can't go out on your own."

Again, Nati smiled. "Oh . . . yeah," he said, as if once more he'd merely forgotten the rules.

I imagine that Nati's teacher started to realize that she was dealing with a unique individual when he snuck out the third time that day.

The fourth time Nati snuck out in a single day doesn't really count since he didn't actually make it outside before he got busted. Nati's teacher told me he was "strutting" as he moved toward the door, confident of his Houdini-like ability to sneak out of class at will. He was having the time of his life . . . right up till he got busted again.

One more "Oh . . . yeah," accompanied by the Nati smile.

Nati was different. There was never any way he was going to be anything but different. Different language. Different way of seeing the world. He'd never been to preschool like all of the other kids in his class. He didn't know the rules and norms. Maybe when you're the only Ethiopian kid in a classroom full of children from Los Angeles, you don't waste much time trying to fit in, but then again, maybe that's just who Nati is and has always been. Either way, I knew pretty early on that Nati was different. He was louder, more confident—well, really more everything—than anyone else I knew. And so I worried.

Which, I guess, is why the chanting was such a big thing.

Almost to the chanting part, really, I am.

One day, long after Nati had given up trying to just walk out of class, I spoke to his teacher to see how he was doing.

"Well," she told me, "he gets very interested in . . . his backside," she tells me.

The Butt-Dance. I'd seen the Butt-Dance. It's what Nati did when he was happy. He'd squat low and shake his butt; sometimes he'd sing, "Uh-huh, uh-huh, eets my birthday, uh-huh, uh-huh."

It occurred to me that I never did tell him not to do the Butt-Dance at school. We had so many things to talk about back then. On the other hand, the Butt-Dance was a big improvement over just leaving. So there was that. (It's only now, years later, that I've come to see the truth. My son Nati was, I'm pretty sure, the inventor of twerking. You're welcome, world.)

And then there was the whole *"Mishashu! A-lubba-lubba"* thing.

There's this song they don't sing in Ethiopia, called *"Mishashu."* When I first met Nati he sang all the time. Back then, it was songs I'd heard before, sort of. There were Amharic versions of "Ring around the Rosy," other songs I half-recognized as old nursery rhyme–type tunes, songs half in English and half in Amharic that he'd been taught at the orphanage. After a while, though, the song we heard the most went like this:

*"Mishashu! A-lubba-lubba."*

Sometimes, Nati would sing *"Mishashu!"* and whoever else in our family who was in the room at the time would sing back, *"A-lubba-lubba."* Other times, he'd sing *"Mishashu!"* and *"A-lubba-lubba."* Sometimes we call it *"the Mishashu song,"* other times we call it *"A-lubba-lubba-la,"* but mostly we call it "the Butt-Dance Song," since it was usually accompanied by Nati's favorite move, the Butt-Dance. Sometimes, to this very day, when I come into the house, I will sing out, *"Mishashu,"* instead of, "Hi, honey, I'm home." Mary, in turn, always answers me with a hearty *"A-lubba-lubba-la."*

I say the *"Mishashu"* song is one they don't sing in Ethiopia because while we had, at first, assumed it was some sort of ditty that was number one on the Ethiopian dance charts, in fact, we've never been able to find anyone else from that country who knows the song. It might be something Nati heard and mangled; it might be something he wrote himself. I don't really know. What I do know is that he liked to sing it an awful lot, pretty much anywhere he was.

My son, I worried, was weird. Awkward. Strange. Some of that was undeniable. He didn't speak English, he sang strange songs, he snuck out of class, he wiggled his butt a whole lot, he tended to miss some social cues. There was, for instance, the time he got introduced to Duck, Duck, Goose at summer camp.

It was his first summer with us. There was a day camp near us, so I enrolled Nati, and for the first few weeks I hung around the camp to translate and help him out. The first time the kids formed a circle for a game of Duck, Duck, Goose, Nati, of course, had no idea what was going on. He stood in the middle of the circle while the other kids impatiently waited for him to get with the program. When a counselor suggested he be the one to walk around the group, patting kids' heads and saying, "Duck, duck, goose," Nati was game but confused. When he finally tapped a kid on the head and said "Goose," the other kid jumped up, but Nati just stood there. As the other kids waited again, a counselor explained the game to Nati one more time. When Nati said "Goose" again, he began to run, and for a moment I breathed a sigh of relief. It took only a moment for both Nati and I to realize that he'd picked a faster kid and that he was going to be caught.

Then, because he saw no reason not to, Nati made the

game a bit easier for himself. Instead of running away from the goose by going around the circle, he ran straight away from the circle, out into the field, laughing as he ran.

He was weird, my new kid, and that worried me.

Okay, the chanting.

We decided to hold Nati's birthday party two weeks before his actual birthday, since, as I mentioned, that falls on Halloween, a day most people have pretty well booked up with trick-or-treating. We hired a guy who calls himself Dan the Man to come and keep the kids busy with party games. We sent out invitations, bought some carrots for the adults, and ordered a Batman cake. Nati was beyond excited. Starting the day after Gracie's party in June, he asked us at least once a day, every day, how long it was going to be until his party. For four months. Believe me when I tell you there's a very good reason why NASA starts the countdowns till their rocket launches ten seconds prior to liftoff and not 120 days before.

Given the whole *"Mishashu"*/Duck, Duck, Goose/walking-out-of-class-when-not-doing-the-Butt-Dance issue, we worried that kids wouldn't come, but in the end, it was a pretty big party; twenty-five or thirty children were there celebrating with Nati. They all brought presents: more stuff, more toys, more junk than Nati had seen in all of his life before coming to America. We sang, blew out candles; really, by and large you could have been there and never have known that there was anything unusual about the party or the guest of honor. There certainly were no clues that the birthday boy had been in America for only five months.

Well, almost. I mean, there was the singing. And the chanting. Which I may have mentioned already.

The singing came early on. A bunch of the kids were lined up, while Dan the Man was setting up a game. One or two of the kids would suddenly yell out, "MISHASHU!" at which point all of the kids then shouted back, "A-lubba-lubba-la," just like we did at home. It's not a song I ever really thought would catch on here in Southern California, but midway through Nati's party, I realized my son was the creator of a musical sensation. Parents told me that not only were Nati's classmates singing the song, but his classmates' siblings were now singing it too. Entire families could now be heard singing "Mishashu."

A few parents wanted to know what the words meant; sadly, I had to inform them that I had no idea what the song was about. A group of us speculated on the possibility that Nati had taught his class to sing a song whose lyrics encouraged them to overthrow the government and install him as our nation's dictator. I'm still not ruling that out, by the way.

A kid walked by, heard the song, and immediately began smacking his own butt (a vital part of the Butt-Dance sequence) and singing "Mishashu," after which Nati and the first kid joined in with an enthusiastic "A-lubba-lubba-la." Then Nati, resuming his rightful place as lead singer, called out "Mishashu!" and the two kids he'd been singing with took their places as backup singers and joined in with their hearty "*A-lubba-lubba-las.*"

Nati started doing the Butt-Dance, bending his knees and wiggling and pointing at his butt. And then they were all doing it. Twenty-five or thirty American kids and my son, singing "*Mishashu, a-lubba-lubba-la,*" while laughing and shaking their booties. Nati in the middle of them all, dancing up a storm.

All of that really should have prepared me for the chanting, but it didn't. The thing of it is, it's hard to know what other kids think of your child. And Nati was clearly a fairly special case. And while kids might have understood that there was a reason why Nati didn't get their games or understand the rules, that doesn't automatically mean that they were going to want to keep playing with him anyway. He picked up soccer balls with his hands during games, ran the wrong way with the football, and pretended to see snakes to distract the opposition when he was playing basketball. When I first started calling the parents of Nati's classmates to make playdates, I made a point of telling them that I'd understand if they'd rather not, since at the time he spoke so little English.

Then, too, I saw Nati through my own prism as his father. I spent so much time having to tell him things over and over, getting him not to shout when he was standing right next to me, showing him how to play—and how not to play—so many games and sports that though I'd heard he was popular at school and that the other kids liked him, I really had no way of knowing for sure what was going on every day after I dropped him off.

And so, that day at Nati's party, the chanting took me by surprise.

The first time it happened was not long after the *"Mishashu"* dance incident. Suddenly, for no reason, all of the kids started chanting Nati's name.

"NA-TI, NA-TI, NA-TI."

I ran over to see what was going on, but there really wasn't anything. They were all just laughing and having fun. Nati was doing . . . well, I don't know what he was doing, but he was there having a ball. And the chanting continued. It was almost his turn to play some game that Dan the Man had set up and all of the kids were chanting Nati's name.

It happened a few times after that. For some reason, someone would start the chant, others would join in, and then they were off.

I have two other children. I've been to a few hundred kids' parties. I've never heard anyone chant a kid's name like that. They weren't being led into the chant. It wasn't because it was Nati's birthday. It wasn't a thing that Dan the Man was doing for all of the kids or that he did at every party for the birthday boy or girl. They weren't taking turns chanting each other's names. They were just . . . chanting. Nati's name.

Chanting.

At first, Mary and I wondered if it was all because Nati was something of a mascot to the other kids, if they were treating him more like a pet than a classmate. And then it hit me.

I'm an idiot.

They were chanting. They loved him. And of course it made sense that they did. Certainly his classmates couldn't have cared less that Nati shouts when he's standing next to people; that's not something that tends to bother the average six-year-old boy. Certainly they didn't mind that he was silly, because to them, Nati was just fun. Lots of fun. He did a mean Butt-Dance, he was always happy, he was always silly; really, what's not to love?

His friends were chanting his name, singing his songs, having a blast being with him.

The problem was me. I'd been so busy trying to be tolerant and accepting that I'd forgotten to even consider celebrating and enjoying. I'd been so worried that Nati was different and therefore bad, I'd been so concerned about his weird dancing and singing and not knowing how to play games the right way, that it had simply never occurred to me that all of those "problems" might actually be good things. I'm so thick and prone to well-meaning parental anxiety that it took actual chanting to make me realize that there are no good traits and there are no bad traits, there is only context.

When I heard a group of children singing Nati's gibberish song and chanting his name, I began to think about all of my reactions to his behavior. Nati will argue with a tree stump. He can come up with ten new and different ways to do something like tie his shoe (or he'll simply leave his sneakers untied, wear them like slippers with his heels sticking out, and insist that he prefers them that way). He will tell you that he's learned a new way to fry an egg from a Web site he found when he should have been sleeping and that this new way to fry an egg is much better than your way of frying an egg, even though he has never fried anything in his life. Usually, he's right.

He is loud, argumentative, assertive, competitive, and more confident of himself than Napoleon ever was.

Think of a list of traits you'd like your child to have. Perhaps you'd like your child to be obedient and listen to you when you tell them something. Perhaps you'd like your child to be good at sharing their toys with other children. Maybe you want your child to be aggressive, a take-charge kid who's a natural leader. Certainly, I had my own lists of character traits I hoped to see in my kids.

Got your list? Okay, now let's imagine that somehow, against all expectations and historical precedents, your kids magically get all the traits you hope they will have. Now what? Are they better or worse suited for life in the world?

Your answer is wrong.

Doesn't matter whether you said your child would be better suited for life if they had all the traits you want them to have, or if you said they'd be worse suited if they were magically transformed into who you wish they'd be. Your. Answer. Is. Wrong.

And right. Your answer is also right.

Because a kid who's quiet, sweet, and obedient is a lovely second-grader to have, but a really lousy head of a start-up company. If you're starting up the next Google or Apple, quiet and obedient are probably not going to be all that useful to you. And if you're hoping for a kid who never takes *no* for an answer, who's always ready to push, argue, and prod his way forward, you better hope they succeed at their start-up, because aggressive go-getters can sometimes struggle when they don't get to be the boss.

There is no character trait that is good or bad. There is only context. We know this as adults. Few people would be really great at being doctors and stand-up comedians, teachers and CEOs, or salespeople and research scientists. For years after hearing Nati's classmates chant his name, I continued to try to mold his character, making him less argumentative, quieter, and more, well, more like me. And when I finally stopped doing that, it was mostly because I'd realized that I simply couldn't change him. And that was good. It was better to accept that than to keep banging my head against the wall. But real peace came to me only when I realized that I didn't have to accept that Nati was who he was, I had to celebrate it.

Nati doesn't need to be any quieter and Clay and Grace don't need to be any louder. What they need is to find the places in life that will work best for them as they are. Hammers are great for driving nails and really lousy when you use them to brush your teeth. (Seriously, they are. Nati's tried.) Same with people.

I can create the correct context moment by moment in our house. Nati likes to argue. That can be a difficult thing sometimes. Grace tends to prefer harmony. That can be pleasant. And yet, during the many hours I spend in the car with my kids, while Grace will pleasantly listen to music, chat with me, or text friends, Nati will be fully and completely engaged. What can be a troublesome quality when I'm trying to get him to do things my way becomes a really wonderful quality as he and I speed down the freeway talking about the news, arguing over what we think and feel, and being 100 percent present with each other.

I can spend my life loving Grace's sweet demeanor, but I can't do that and then get upset when she's quiet on long car rides. I can be upset that Nati is raucous and argumentative, but I'd never want to give up our long, passionate discussions about sports and politics and how to live, all of which sometimes seem to happen because he simply can't not engage.

Not long ago, Clay and I were looking at colleges. Every college presentation seems to fit the same template. You walk onto the campus and sit in an auditorium. The admissions office gives an hour-long talk about their college and what makes it unique. Then you take a tour of the campus with an actual student. The hour-long talk will make you feel like the school you are seeing is the most remarkable institute of higher education that has ever existed. The campus tour you take will be equally remarkable and the student conducting it will, without fail, be the most charming, delightful young adult you have ever seen. I took Clay to about a dozen colleges. We have been on tours conducted by young men and women, and I would gladly have any of my children marry any of them because they were all just that good. Harry Potter and Hogwarts would have nothing on these kids and these schools.

And yet, a few hours after the tour, after we're done oohing and aahing over the ivy-covered walls or the unique urban campus, Clay and I always found ourselves pausing and thinking a little more. It's not that we doubted the schools were wonderful, it's that we began to notice that they might or might not be wonderful for him. Ivy-covered walls are great, unless you want to live in the middle of a city. Cities are great, unless your heart is set on ivy-covered walls. There are great schools in this world, of course, just as there are schools that aren't great. But among all the schools that we looked at, the question was only which school was great for Clay. It's the same when it comes to the traits that make up who we are. It's not so much that it's good to be quiet or bad to be gregarious; it's only a question of what fits the moment or the people with us in that moment.

Unfortunately most people, especially kids, can't change who they are to fit different moments. I'm not very good at math, so I tend to avoid situations where I'll be asked to do long division. You can do that when you're an adult. Kids can't. Loud kids can't suddenly quiet down for school. Shy, studious kids can't suddenly burst out with vivacious enthusiasm when it's time to make new friends or be more aggressive when they switch from math class to gym. Seeing all those schools with Clay reminded me that often what can seem either good or bad is really just either good or bad depending on people's taste or mood or just on the moment.

Consider my own father's story.

My dad grew up a nice Jewish boy in New York. Every day of his childhood, his parents told him that he should grow up to be a nice Jewish doctor. There were always going to be sick people in this world, and so doctors would always be able to make a living. Be a doctor, they told him, and so he listened. When it came time to go to school, he went into premed.

Sadly, a few problems came up. The first was that my father had no head for science. He worked hard in his chemistry classes but just couldn't master the subject. Still, he might have made a go of it but for the other, slightly larger problem.

My father hates sick people. And blood. People who sneeze horrify him, people who cough upset him deeply, and the sight of blood makes him grow pale. And let's not even start with how upset he'd be if he had to treat a sick person who was also bleeding.

So the whole premed thing didn't go so well.

My father didn't quit.

He had spent his whole life hearing about how happy he and his parents would be if only he became a doctor. True, he was clearly not good at learning the things doctors need to know, and true, he really couldn't stand being around sick people, but no one had ever told my dad that he had to become a *good* doctor; they'd only said he had to become a doctor, and so he came up with another plan.

I'm embarrassed to say it.

I think perhaps the best way to work my way into this part of the story is to say that my father meant no harm. Or rather, he meant no harm that he thought was all that important.

My father grew up a poor kid in a tiny apartment in New York, and so he had no pets as a child. He hates animals almost as much as he hates sick people, so he really didn't understand that people get very attached to their dogs and cats and other pets. Which is why, when he realized that he wasn't going to be all that good at being a doctor, he decided to become a veterinarian.

Actually, it kind of makes sense. In a way.

See, he figured if he couldn't get someone's dog to feel better, it wouldn't be that big a deal. It was just a dog, right?

Being a vet also didn't work out. Again, given that he hates blood, illness, animals, and chemistry, that wasn't a big surprise.

So my father, beaten and discouraged and convinced he'd never amount to anything, began to study things that actually, you know, interested him. He loves food and he loves finance, so he became an expert in the financial ins and outs of food companies. He got very engrossed in finance, which my grandfather didn't understand or trust at all, and found that he was well suited for it. And now, as I write this, he's eighty years old and still working in that field, happy as a clam. He has a lovely office, which is to him a playground. Best of all, he is able to continue to avoid blood, germs, animals, and science.

It seems clear to me that my father doesn't need to like sick people or chemistry and that Clay doesn't need to like schools located in cities instead of schools with big campuses (or vice versa). My father just needed to find the job that matched who he was. Same with Clay and schools, and yes, same with all three of my kids and who they are.

Nati is loud and raucous and had no problems finding kids his age who loved those qualities. I'm quieter and more suited to things like writing. For me to believe that Nati needs to be different or would be better off in life if he were only a little more of this and a little less of that is the sort of insanity that is born of the desperate combination of fear and love that exists every moment of every day in most every parent. We love our kids so much that we can't help but want to tinker, to improve them ever so slightly for their own good.

The fact that Nati's classmates loved him enough to chant his name on his birthday surprised me, but really it shouldn't have. He was the perfect six-year-old to all those other six-year-old kids. And when I remember that all of my children's qualities are capable of taking them to the exact correct destination for them, then something truly remarkable happens to me.

I lose my fear.

I remember all the love that was behind the fear.

And sometimes, I even remember to lead the chants for them myself.

# GRANDPARENT YOUR KIDS

---

*How Mom and Dad Two Times Taught Me*

*How to Happily Love My Kids*

T'S HARD TO WRITE ABOUT NATI AND HIS RELATIONSHIP with my parents. That's not because they have a bad relationship, or because they rejected him or he them. It's hard to write about it because absolutely everything to do with the subject is just so weird, I don't really know where to begin.

Honestly, I always found my parents' relationship with all three of my kids strange. My parents would come out for a visit with gifts for the kids. My dad would play catch with Clay and both my parents would patiently and lovingly read to the kids and play games with them for hours. I, on the other hand, would sit and watch this multigenerational bonding festival and think to myself, "Who are these old people and when will the people who raised me be coming by for a visit?"

Still, I had more than the usual amount of concern before Nati met my parents. Nati had, after all, been passed from his mother's home to his grandmother's home before finally landing at the orphanage. Finding out my parents were coming into town could have been cause for panic for Nati, since he might easily have thought that we were passing him on to them.

Then, too, there was the fact that my parents had been against our adopting a child. They'd worried that Clay would struggle with that much change. They'd been concerned that we'd be adding an unknown quantity into our lives. They worried that our newest child wouldn't bond with us or our kids.

Throw in the fact that my mother was about to have a black Ethiopian in the family after spending my entire life frantically trying to find a nice Jewish girl for me to marry so that I could give her nice Jewish grandchildren and, yeah, there was a lot going on there.

I asked my parents to hold off on visiting for a while so that Nati could adjust to his new surroundings and then, because of Nati's past, I tried to be extra clear about what would be happening. I told Nati that my parents would be visiting; that they would stay for a few days and then they would go back on the airplane, but that Mom and Dad and Clay and Grace and Nati would all stay in our house and not go with them. Not knowing the Amharic word for "grandpa" or "grandma," I told him that the people who were coming were "Daddy's daddy and Daddy's mommy." Nati, in turn, began referring to my parents as "Daddy Two Times and Mommy Two Times."

And with that bit of clarity achieved, Mommy Two Times and Daddy Two Times, a set of nicknames perhaps better suited for use by Elizabeth Taylor's grandchildren than our kids, came to visit.

They arrived bearing gifts for all of their grandchildren, including comic books designed to teach young people about U.S. monetary policies and the Federal Reserve System. I realize that may sound like an odd joke, but apparently they'd stumbled across the books on a trip to Washington, D.C. My mother is, more than anything else, a practical woman; to her all comic books are essentially the same. Thus, it made sense to her that if children liked reading about Batman and Robin, it would follow that they'd thrill to see the comic adventures of the chairman of the Federal Reserve and his lively cohorts. My parents' trip to the Fed yielded one other gift for each of my children: three small green bundles, one for each kid. The bundles were held together by thin plastic wrap and were each about the size of a short, thickish candle. Each contained a few hundred dollars' worth of thoroughly shredded five-, ten-, and twenty-dollar bills. Apparently, as my mother explained to us all, when a bill has been in circulation for too long and begins to fray, it is destroyed and then sold to elderly tourists who have not yet heard of video games. I have not been able to figure out why the Fed doesn't shred the monetary policy comic books and keep the old bills, but I like to believe better minds than mine are at work on that one.

The kids dutifully thanked their grandparents, and at once Nati began trying to unwrap the shredded bills, which would have resulted in the sort of mess that would have been very hard to explain to the neighbors. The shredded money was removed and everyone did their best to settle into a normal visit.

If only anyone involved had been anything resembling normal. Start with my mom.

My mother's demands that I marry a Jewish girl started
when I was nine and still thought all girls, Jewish or not, were
"gross." Those demands continued through my teens, into
my early adulthood, and up until I met the woman who is
now my wife. As it happens, my wife's name is Mary, and, also
as it happens, my Jewish grandmother's name was Mary.
Thus, when I told my mother that I had met and fallen in love
with a girl named Mary, she gulped audibly on the phone and
then asked, "Is that Mary as in the Virgin Mary, or as in
Grandma Mary?"

"Well," I replied with an audible gulp of my own, "hopefully neither."

But in truth, it was Mary as in Grandma Mary, since my new girlfriend was, like Grandma Mary, Jewish.

Of course, marrying Mary only subtly altered my mother's demands. With the dexterity usually associated with three-card monte dealers, my mother quickly shifted and began to insist that what was most important in my life was that I spawn Jewish grandchildren who would one day go on to be bar or bat mitzvahed. Perhaps my memory is playing cruel tricks on me, but I'm reasonably certain my mother's gift to my wife and me on our first wedding anniversary was to offer to pay for a bris in the event that my wife became pregnant with a son.

When Mary and I decided to adopt a child, I took pains to be gentle with my parents. I consciously avoided jokes or any hint of sarcasm, and slowly and softly answered any question they had. When my parents warned me that adopting a child who didn't speak English was going to be "hard," I did not give in to the temptation to say, "It's going to be hard? Raising a child? Really? I had no idea. To hell with it, then," and instead simply nodded and waited for the next question.

I also didn't bother bringing up the fact that Nati was not the first person in our family to have been adopted.

During the years before World War II, my mother's father and mother were living in Belgium. One of my mother's few memories of her parents is of her mother sewing a yellow Jewish star on her father's clothes. It was the star that all Jews were made to wear after the Nazis took power; it was the star that would, in time, make clear which people were to be exterminated. One of my mother's other memories of her parents is of the day they left her behind.

Her parents had arranged for her to be taken through the Resistance underground to a Catholic boarding school. The nuns there had agreed to take in about twenty Jewish children and hide them from the Nazis. My mother, born Rachel Szmulewicz, was given a new name, Monique Simonis, and told that she was never to tell anyone, ever, that she was Jewish. Not far from the orphanage was an SS camp. Had any of the SS officers found out my mother's real last name, she, too, would have been given a yellow star; she, too, would have been killed. She was, at the time they parted, four years old.

My grandparents gave my mother to the nuns, knowing they would almost certainly never see her again. When the underground found out that the SS camp was going to raid the school to look for Jewish children being hidden, my mother and the other Jewish children were snuck out. My mother, then still a young child, remembers only that she was thrilled to get to sleep in a real bed.

The nuns who raised my mother were hardly enlightened in their treatment of the children; when a student wet the bed, they were forced to wear the soiled sheets around their necks throughout the following day, but they kept my mother alive throughout the war at the greatest possible risk to their own lives. My Jewish mother was raised until she was nine by the nuns; she attended church services and was, for all purposes, a practicing Catholic. When one of the girls at the school told a nun that she, too, hoped to follow that path when she grew up, the nun said, "No, you won't become a nun; that will be Monique."

When the American soldiers came and liberated my mother's country, a few of the other Jewish children were picked up by their parents. My mother has a memory of that, too; she was taken out with a friend whose parents had come back for her. They had lunch. My mother's friend went home with her parents; my mother returned to the orphanage. Her parents did not come. Years later, my mother learned they'd died at the concentration camp in Auschwitz.

In time, my mother's uncle and his wife, now living in America, adopted my mother. She remembers the trip over by boat; a nine-year-old girl who spoke no English traveling across the ocean alone. Coming into America, nearing Ellis Island, they passed by the Statue of Liberty. When the boat approached the dock, the various immigrants meeting the boat began to throw bananas and apples toward the people onboard, to show them that they had at last come to a land with enough food, where they could live a good life. The history of skilled Jewish athletes being a short one, most of the food fell far short of the boat. My mother remembers being angry at the waste, and laughs now about how she wanted to jump into the water to get the food before it sank.

She was raised by her aunt Mary and her uncle Max. Their kindness was largely limited to taking her in; my mother was in charge of caring for her younger "sister," the woman I grew up calling my aunt, who was in reality my mother's younger cousin. When she went to school in America, on her first day, a boy whispered to her that he'd heard there was someone in the class who was from Europe; my mother, still not overly anxious to be found, whispered back, "Who ez it?" in her thick Belgian accent.

When my mother was in her twenties, she met and married my father. My sister was their first child; my mother named her new daughter Jeanine Monique, so that her children would never forget their mother's story. When I came along, she proposed that I be named Claude Simonis, but my father, New York City born and bred, put his foot down and insisted that I simply be called Claude S. Knobler, fearing that any boy named Claude Simonis would almost certainly not give him a daughter-in-law or grandchildren.

When I was very young, my mother told me that my marrying a Jewish girl was how we would make sure the Nazis didn't "win." I, in turn, explained to her that the Nazis had already clearly and indisputably lost the war, and that I intended to marry whomever I fell in love with. I grew up, dated women of various religions, and then accidentally fell in love with Mary, as in Grandma and not the Virgin Mary. My mother was very gracious about not gloating in front of me.

My father, on the other hand, grew up in New York. His father was a tailor and his family was very poor. My dad believed that being a father meant paying the bills. We did spend

time together, to be sure, but we were and are different people, of different generations. He worried a great deal about
how I'd do in the world and tended to do a lot of that worrying out loud. He was born during the Depression, had relatives killed in the Holocaust, and worked without pause to
build the sort of life he wanted to live and that he thought
would be best for my sister and me. It would be far from accurate to depict him as cold or distant, but I think he won't
mind if I do say that when I was growing up he frequently
told my sister and me that kids, while great, didn't really become interesting to talk to until just before they were old
enough to leave the house for good.

I had a few doubts about how well the visit with Nati
might work out.

Once again, my fears could not have been more misguided. My parents adored Nati. Nati adored my parents. I
watched them read together, make drawings together, and
laugh and play with each other. Of course, I really and truly
knew that Nati was part of the family when, on the second
day of their visit, I overheard my mother say to her new
grandson, "And one day, you'll grow up and then you'll marry
a nice Jewish girl."

Nati had no idea what she was saying, of course. But he
adored "Mom Two Times" and "Dad Two Times," these two
strange old people who were being so nice to him, so he
smiled his biggest smile, nodded his head, and said, "K . . .
k . . . o-kee." I knew then and there, that the kid was in.

What has proved to be even stranger than hearing my mother telling her non-English-speaking Ethiopian grandson that he'd grow up and marry a nice Jewish girl has been seeing the relationship that my father and Nati have forged. My parents have five grandchildren and they love all of them fiercely, but there's no doubt in my mind that of all five grandchildren, Nati is the one who most resembles my father. Nati is obsessed with stocks and bonds. When he was less than ten years old, he began picking out stocks for his own portfolio, which my father helped him manage. When they are together, the two of them sit and discuss finance and the global economy.

Nati, it turns out, is the son my father never had.

Again, that's not to say that my dad doesn't love me, or my sister, Jeanine, or Clay or Grace or my nieces, Jessie and Sarah. He does. But the connection he shares with Nati is remarkable. And, well, remarkably funny. They are two oddly identical peas in a pod.

My father, in his own inimitable style, assures me that the reason why he and his grandchildren have bonded so closely is that in me, they share a common enemy, but I'm not buying it. I look at the connection my parents share with my children, and what I always see is love unencumbered. My parents have consciously decided that it is not their job to ensure that my children grow up to be responsible, tidy, efficient, high-achieving superhumans. That's my job. Their job is just to enjoy.

Okay, enjoy and also convince all three of my kids to

marry Jewish people. I mean, some things are too important to be left to chance.

Love unencumbered. Having decided that it's not their job to mold my children into who they think they should be, my parents have become free to love them for exactly who they are. My father connects with Nati about money, with Clay about sports, and with Grace about her love for his hometown, New York City. My mother is the same, except that she connects with the several mountains of food she prepares for each child when we visit.

Were I to say that we should love our children as if they were all grandchildren, it would sound recklessly irresponsible. I know that parents have more responsibilities than grandparents. But I also know that the experience of adopting and raising a five-year-old child has taught me beyond all doubt that my children are there to be loved and not molded, celebrated for who they are and not for who I plan on making them. Raising Nati has made it clear that when I stop trying to control their futures, I'm not really letting go of control at all. All I can truly let go of is the illusion of control. Nati is who he is. So is Clay. So is Grace. And who they are is perfect. Why not enjoy them?

I have seen a mother give her child away knowing that his only chance for life was to go far from her home, so perhaps I know a small bit of what my own grandparents were thinking the day they gave my mother over to the nuns. They could not have imagined any of it, of course; my mother at the Catholic school, her meeting my father, the children they would have, and the strange and prosperous country they would raise them in. They could not have dreamed that their child would become a grandmother, let alone would they have ever imagined that one day she'd have this grandson, a black child who spoke neither French nor English. He is their great-grandson, though, a part of their legacy. That is, in the end, what family is: the people we are connected to, by blood, by marriage, and sometimes by choice.

Most of all, we are connected by love. Today, I can choose to express that love as fear, as the demand that my children grow along a certain plan toward the goals I have chosen for them. Or I can accept the limits of my power and simply love them as they are.

Nati has made that choice both more and less complicated. Forming a family out of such dissimilar parts has not always been a graceful process, but it has given me an overwhelming sense of clarity about what works and what doesn't. Fear, no matter how well intentioned, has never once changed any of my children or helped them grow toward becoming the men and woman they can one day be. Love, on the other hand, has never failed me. When I love and accept my children as they are, I don't have to shout for quiet and I don't have to try to nag, punish, and force people into mature responsibility. Love is what I put my faith in, scary though that may be.

My family, so unexpected, so very different than I could have ever planned, has turned out to be the perfect family for me. For Mary, for Clay, for Grace, for Nati, and for the people whose selfless love for Nati showed me a path I might never have known, I am, and will forever be, truly grateful. There is no family that is not, in its own way, a miracle. Perhaps if Mary and I hadn't adopted Nati I might not have noticed that as often as I do, but it would be no less true. And therein lies the greatest secret of all. The miracle has already happened. All we have to do is never lose sight of it.

# FAMILY
# PHOTOS

STILL HAVE THE FIRST PICTURE I EVER SAW OF MY SON. IT'S only a little bigger than a postage stamp, the sort of photo you might use for a passport picture. It's not a great picture and it really doesn't do Nati justice as he was then, or as he is now. I nearly threw it away when I first got it. Now I treasure it.

I still have some of the pictures the orphanage sent me of Nati before he came to America, too. There's the one of him laughing during a party with two of his friends, and another of him smiling as he holds the bag of toys and pictures we sent him so that he'd know he had a new family. Years after that picture was taken, Nati told us that the older kids had taken the toy cars from him. It's hard to think of that without wanting to run out and buy him a toy car right now, but of course, Nati is a teenager and the car he wants me to buy him now isn't a toy.

Of course, most of the pictures I have of Nati were taken after he came home with me. Those are the pictures I really treasure. There's the photo of Nati meeting Mary, Grace, and Clay for the first time, just after our plane landed. He's smiling ear to ear and we're all hugging each other and laughing, none of us having the slightest idea of all that would happen in the years, or even days, ahead.

After that, the photos start looking a lot more like everyone else's family snapshots. Well, close to how everyone else's pictures look, I guess. There's Nati dressed as Elvis for Halloween and tons of pictures from more than ten years of birthday parties and vacations. I have pictures of first days at school and grade-school graduation days. There are photos of the kids playing sports, eating together, and just hanging out.

I love all of the pictures I've got. I have pictures of Clay taken long before Nati was born. Clay was a shy, sweet, quiet little guy; now, he's a confident, funny young man. He and Nati used to share a room. Neither of them told me while it was happening, but in Nati's first few years here, he used to leave his bed in the middle of the night more often than not, and climb into Clay's small bed for a few hours so he could feel safe in the dark. Maybe that's how Clay learned to nurture and grew into the man he is today. Then again, maybe he was always going to be that person. Either way, Clay became less shy and became a big brother who was fiercely determined to help look after his siblings at school and with friends. We watch football, baseball, and basketball together and he is effortlessly funny and always kind.

It's a funny thing about kids. When they're young, you're the center of their world. They want you to watch them when they go down the slide, they want you to be next to them wherever they are, and they think you hung the moon. Then, one day, when you're far too busy to notice, your roles re-

verse. Mary and I and every parent of every high school senior we know all get excited when our eighteen-year-olds have time to hang around with us, and yet we know that the time we do spend together is much more exciting for us than it is for them. The pictures I take of Clay now look like the sort of photos fans take with movie stars. Clay is smiling patiently, while Mary and I grin like lunatics. Sometimes I catch myself wanting to tell the exhausted parents of young children to enjoy these times; they'll go by quicker than they think. And then I remember all the sleepless nights and the hours of playing dull board games and I just smile.

In the pictures I take of Clay these days, he always seems to be wearing a Duke University sweatshirt. He started there as a freshman in the fall. I'm already planning on visiting far too often.

When we'd first started talking about adopting a child, Grace was still wearing princess dresses and taking ballet classes with other preschoolers; now she's babysitting other parents' little kids. When Nati first arrived, he tended to focus more of his attention on Clay than on Grace. We worried about that (we worried about everything), but Grace never seemed to mind. "That's okay," she'd reassure her mother and me, "Clay and Nati both like sports and things like that, so it makes sense that Nati would focus on him." Sometime over the years, though, Nati and Grace formed their own bonds. I take pictures of them both and they both roll their eyes at me every time I do. Grace is one year ahead of Nati in school. She's already thinking about all sorts of colleges, some in big cities, some in small towns, and some in Europe. Wherever she winds up, she'll be fine. She, too, has become a confident, intelligent adult. I wish I could take the credit, but when I look at all my photos of her, of her being kind and loving toward Nati before she even knew him, of her exploring new places and new things, I realize that she's always been the same delightful, smart, confident, and loving person she is now. I'm just glad I got to be there while it all happened.

I suppose this could be amazing only to someone who spent the last decade at home raising kids, but the most recent pictures I took of Mary and me were of the two of us walking on the beach, alone with no kids in sight, on our first child-

free vacation in years. Somehow, this year when spring break came around, all three of our kids were doing their own thing. Grace and Nati were participating in service trips with their school. Clay had been invited to travel with a friend's family. And so Mary and I made the best of it and took off on our own to do next to nothing on a quiet beach. When your kids are young, it's hard not to feel like your marriage is a business partnership. Deciding who watches the kids and who gets to take a shower or have a cup of coffee can be a wee bit stressful, but it turns out now that our kids have busy lives of their own, Mary and I still really love hanging out together. Years ago, my father told me that empty-nest syndrome was actually a lot of fun. I can't say Mary and I are looking forward to those days, but we sure aren't dreading them all the time either.

And Nati? Well, I took a picture of him just this morning, as a matter of fact. Mary still works at an office, so years ago I got into the habit of taking pictures on my phone and e-mailing them so she could see the kids having breakfast and find out what they were wearing that day to school (actually, I'm pretty sure Mary had me start doing that to make sure I was braiding Grace's hair correctly, way back when. There were days when, after I'd finished doing her pigtails, she looked very much like a unicorn). In the picture I took this morning, Nati looks pretty damn elegant. He's wearing a V-neck sweater, tan slacks, and an expression of bemused annoyance at being photographed once again. I'm not entirely sure where or even when Nati picked up his fashion sense, but while I went to high school dressed in old jeans and T-shirts, Nati, as always, has his own way of going about things. He is now, as he has always been, a confident and charismatic wonder. Of course, he is not the same person he was when he first came home with me at age five, and of course, he is. He still likes to tease and surprise me. When he was five he did that by running ahead of me in our hotel in Ethiopia, hiding and then jumping out and yelling, "Yes!" Now, he likes to argue politics with me instead. We debate, laugh, exasperate, and love each other, and I wouldn't have it any other way.

There are pictures of Nati's mother in my house as well. I see them, and I remember the day we met, the day she gave her son to me, knowing she was too ill to raise him herself. My world, and my family's world, is as big as the globe. We are each of us connected, in our own different ways, to the woman in that picture; connected to the sadness in her eyes, the hope in her heart, the trust she placed in us all.

There is another photograph in my house, just as important as all the others, even though it is of a man I never met. In the picture, he's sitting in a hospital bed, his head propped up on his arm. He has a mustache and a confident smile. The photo was taken after his car accident, just after the blood transfusion that gave him the illness that led to his death. There are crutches near the bed, a radio and a thermos of water by his side. It's the only photo Nati has of his father. I think of Nati's father often, and of the son we share. I am mindful of my responsibility to him, and so, too, I am forever aware, because of him, that having children is a great privilege. I have struggled and made mistakes, but I have never forgotten that more than anything else, my children, all three of them, are there to be cherished and loved, perfect today as they are in their photographs, perfect today as they were the day they were born.

## ACKNOWLEDGMENTS

More than anyone else, I'd like to thank and acknowledge Johnny Depp, Jennifer Aniston, and the entire Kardashian family for their help in turning this book from an idea into a reality.

True, I've never met Johnny Depp, Jennifer Aniston, or any of the thousands of people who are in the Kardashian family/empire, but I do still want to thank them, if only because it is my fervent hope that seeing their names here will convince you to continue to read this short chapter. No kidding, if it takes the glamor of some celebrity name-dropping to get people to join me in appreciating the people I do know and who I'm about to name, then you can look forward to a few more movie stars, or at least their names, any minute now.

The point is, I know it's easy to skip the acknowledgments. Sad to say, I often have in the past, but only because until now, I had no idea how much some people truly deserve to be acknowledged.

My editor, Sara Carder, saw an essay I'd written for Dr. Jane Aronson's book, *Carried in Our Hearts*, and asked if I might like to write a book myself. Would I like to write a book? Uh . . . yes, since I was seven. Seriously, what author gets lucky like that? Had she not found me and worked with me and seen me through this process, I'd be exactly what I was when I was seven—a guy who'd like to write a book someday. I am deeply in her debt, not only for asking me to write this book, but also for working so long on it with me.

It has also been my great good fortune to have gotten to work with my agent, Lindsay Edgecombe. Intelligent, generous with her time, insightful, and indispensible; I urge you to buy multiple copies of this book if only so that Lindsay and Sara can be more fairly compensated for all their efforts, kindness, and skill.

And then there are my family and friends. The people I am closest to, who are, without doubt, entirely worthy of acknowledgment both in these pages and out in the world.

Jennifer Lawrence and Leonardo DiCaprio, for example. And really, I'll be thanking all sorts of other celebrities I don't know in just a moment, so do please keep reading. Honest!

I have to thank my sister, Jeanine Nadler, not only because I love her with all my heart, not only for the hours she's spent listening to me talk about this book and who knows what else, not only for her warmth and wit and love, but because she's my big sister and if I don't thank her, I assume she'll crush me like a bug, as is her big-sister prerogative. So, too, must I thank Jeanine's family: Dan, Jessie, and Sarah, not because they've ever done anything to help me but because Dan's her husband and Jessie and Sarah are my nieces and now that I've mentioned them, how cool a brother in-law/uncle am I?

My mother and father are discussed in these pages, so I hope they already know how grateful I am for all they've given me. Honestly, I wouldn't mention them again here, but I assume nobody but my parents will actually read the acknowledgments.

Well, them and people who want to read about celebrities. Tom Hanks! Tom Cruise! Thanks to you both!

Paul Halpern was my best man the day I got married, and has been my best friend since near the dawn of time. I have depended on him for help, wisdom, and support on a near-constant basis for three decades. Really. We spoke less than ten minutes ago as of this writing and whatever thin grasp I have on sanity in this world, I owe, in part, to him.

So, too, am I grateful for all that the late Larry Gelbart gave to me in counsel, humor, and help.

Finally, I have found nothing in this book more challenging to write than these short paragraphs you're about to read here in the acknowledgments.

I am, I'm afraid, not nearly articulate enough to make clear just how grateful I am to my family. I have never met anyone who did not fall in love with my wife, Mary, within minutes of meeting her. She is kind, loving, decent, witty, and beautiful, and every friend I have, as well as my own parents, has made it abundantly clear to me that the luckiest day I ever had in my life was the day she married me. I am not acknowledging her here for her help with this book, though certainly she was a help in writing this book, but rather for the support she has given me in every conceivable way in the over two decades I have known and loved her.

So, too, must I thank each of my children. I am profoundly grateful to Clay, Grace, and Nati for letting me tell our story in this book, and far more than that, for letting me share in their lives. They are each, in their own ways, the most remarkable people I've ever met. I am gleefully astonished on a daily basis by the way they live their lives and the greatest joy I have lies in watching them do just that. They are each possessing of more courage, humor, and gentleness of spirit than anyone else I've ever known.

Finally, I thank and acknowledge Nati's parents, whom, I hope and pray, smile on all I do as I know that they do for the son we share.

If you enjoyed this book, visit

**www.tarcherbooks.com**

and sign up for Tarcher's e-newsletter to receive
special offers, giveaway promotions, and
information on hot upcoming releases.

### TARCHER
### PENGUIN

*Great Lives Begin with Great Ideas*

## Connect with the Tarcher Community

• • •

Stay in touch with favorite authors!
Enter weekly contests!
Read exclusive excerpts!
Voice your opinions!

### Follow us

 Tarcher Books

@TarcherBooks

If you would like to place a bulk order
of this book, call 1-800-847-5515.

# ALSO FROM TARCHER

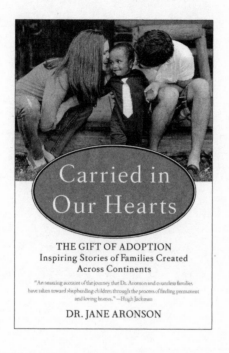

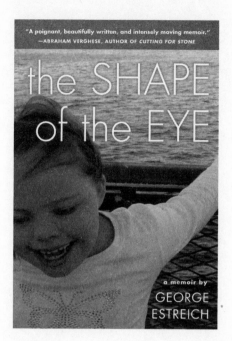

"A poignant, beautifully written, and intensely moving memoir."
—ABRAHAM VERGHESE, AUTHOR OF *CUTTING FOR STONE*

the SHAPE
of the EYE

a memoir by
GEORGE
ESTREICH

"In this wise and moving memoir, George Estreich tells the story of his family as his younger daughter is diagnosed with Down syndrome and they are thrust into an unfamiliar world. Estreich writes with a poet's eye and gift of language, weaving this personal journey into the larger history of his family, exploring the deep and often hidden connections between the past and the present. Engaging and unsentimental, *The Shape of the Eye* taught me a great deal. It is a story I found myself thinking about long after I'd finished the final pages."

—KIM EDWARDS,
author of *The Memory Keeper's Daughter*

978-0-39916-334-0
$16.95